WHOLE BRAIN TEACHING

122

Amazing Games!

Challenging Kids, Classroom Management,
Writing, Reading, Math,
Common Core/State Tests

CHRIS BIFFLE

Director, Whole Brain Teachers of America

Also by Christopher Biffle

A Guided Tour of Five Works by Plato (McGraw-Hill)

A Guided Tour of Descartes' Meditations on First Philosophy (McGraw-Hill)

A Guided Tour of Aristotle's Nicomachean Ethics (McGraw-Hill)

Landscape of Wisdom: An Introduction to Philosophy (McGraw-Hill)

Castle of the Pearl: A Guide to Self Knowledge (HarperCollins)

A Journey Through Your Childhood (Tarcher)

The Garden in the Snowy Mountains: Self Exploration With Jesus As Your Guide (HarperCollins)

Whole Brain Teaching for Challenging Kids (Whole Brain Teaching Press)

*Remembering, in delight, the long walks
when you improved my stories,
this book is dedicated to
my daughter,
Saskia*

We learn by going, where we have to go.

— THEODORE ROETHKE

"The best thing for being sad," replied Merlin, beginning to puff and blow, "is to learn something. That's the only thing that never fails. You may grow old and trembling in your anatomies, you may lie awake at night listening to the disorder of your veins, you may miss your only love, you may see the world about you devastated by evil lunatics, or know your honor trampled in the sewers of baser minds. There is only one thing for it then — to learn. Learn why the world wags and what wags it. That is the only thing which the mind can never exhaust, never alienate, never be tortured by, never fear or distrust, and never dream of regretting. Learning is the only thing for you. Look what a lot of things there are to learn."

— T.H. WHITE, *The Once and Future King*

Book design: Lucinda Geist

WholeBrainTeaching.com

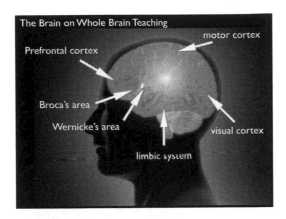

Prefrontal cortex: The brain's reasoning center, activated during decision making. For example, when students devise plans to climb levels on the *Super Improvers Team*, a fundamental WBT game, the prefrontal cortex is powerfully engaged.

Motor cortex: Along with other brain regions, the motor cortex via the hippocampus directs the body's physical movement. *Mirror Words*, one of WBT's most popular strategies, involves the motor cortex in transferring information from short term memory to long term memory.

Visual cortex: One of the brain's largest regions, the visual cortex processes input from the eyes and stores visual memories. WBT's *Scoreboard* and most of its other games, provide strong visual, learning reinforcements.

Limbic system: the brain's emotional core. Virtually every game in *122 Amazing Games!* activates the limbic system, linking academic information to long lasting memory cues.

Wernicke's area, Broca's area: Understanding spoken language (Wernicke's area) and producing spoken language (Broca's area) are continuously involved during *Teach-Okay*, WBT's primary instructional technique.

Begin your journey through 122 Amazing Games! with reflections about your teaching experience.

My main instructional problems are: _Keeping students motivated and attentive_

Solutions I have tried are: _Change of routine, voice reflection, and having students move and be involved_

My strengths as an educator are: _Flexible, organized, Student/teacher relationship._

Areas of personal, instructional growth in this next year will be: _Working on changing my behavior in the classroom to improve student success_

Ron Clark academy _Harry Potter Theme_

Contents

First Words

In dreams begin responsibilities.

—W.B. YEATS

American students have been the victims of a deeply injurious educational system for more than 30 years. In 1983, President Reagan introduced *A Nation At Risk*, a scathing evaluation of U.S. schools. The report declared, "If an unfriendly foreign power had attempted to impose on America the mediocre educational performance that exists today, we might well have viewed it as an act of war."

In 2013, the National Education Association asserted, "Many of the problems identified in 1983 remain unaddressed, and stagnant student achievement continues to challenge educators and administrators."

According to the 2012 Nation's Report Card, average math and reading scores for 17-year-olds have remained relatively unchanged since the 1970s. The Huffington Post reports, "America's high school seniors have mostly stagnated on the National Assessment of Education Progress in reading and math."

Terrible as this is, there's worse news. An article in the New York Times points out a statistic that should make our nation's leaders tremble... suspension rates, kindergarten through high school, *have nearly doubled from the early 1970s through 2006*. Whatever is happening with our test scores, something else, something catastrophic, is going on in our schools. As countless teachers across America can testify, disruptive kids are hijacking our classrooms.

I talk to thousands of educators every year. I ask, "What is your class like, when your most disruptive child is absent?" The teachers' response is so joyful, you would think I had announced a salary increase. *My challenging kid is absent? I can teach! Halleloo! Halleloo!*

It is certainly true that no child should be left behind. A greater truth is that no child should be permitted to hold other children behind.

Our nation's education experts are missing the point. Reading is not the problem. Math proficiency is not the problem. Test scores, which everyone obsesses over, are not the problem. The problem is that disruptive students are driving teachers batty. One third of all new teachers leave after three years; almost half bail out in five years. Every day, this should be the newspaper headline:

Nation Erupts In Chaos
Challenging kids chase thousands of new teachers over schoolyard fences

The great ship of U.S. education is not dead in the water, it is sinking beneath the sea. Your classroom is a lifeboat. All around you, children thrash among dark waves.

Yearly, millions are spent on educational research. Publishers churn out thousands of glossy textbooks, districts invest in truckloads of computers, teachers create reams of instructional plans, but all is for naught, if students could care less about their lessons.

It doesn't matter what we do in classrooms, if pupils are staring out the windows. It doesn't help if some of our most energetic kids exclaim, "Hey look! What's going on outside?!"

Whole Brain Teaching's solution is simple: *student engagement is at its highest, when kids have a ball learning.* If it's not fun, it's not Whole Brain Teaching. As you'll discover in the pages ahead, we've found lots of ways to have fun.

Founded by three Southern California teachers in 1999, Whole Brain Teaching (WBT) is happily employed by instructors across America and in 200 foreign countries. In the last 15 years, over 40,000 educators have attended our free conferences. WBT YouTube videos have received over 5,000,000 views. More than 15,000,000 pages of free eBooks have been downloaded from WholeBrainTeaching.com.

We've been blessed with great teachers. Co-founders of WBT, Chris Rekstad, Jay Vanderfin and Andrea Schindler took my college techniques and, with remarkable creativity, adapted them to elementary classrooms. After Jason Pedersen, our brilliant programmer, created our website, we were joined by a dazzling group of educators: Jeff Battle (North Carolina), Deb Weigel (Arizona), Farrah Shipley (Texas), Nancy Stoltenberg and Melissa Ortuno (California), Kate Bowski (Delaware), Lindsey Roush (Ohio), Sarah Meador (Illinois), Jasselle Cirino (Pennsylvania), Andre Deshotel (Louisiana), Jackie Nessuno (New Jersey), Liann Nutini (Canada), Michelle Shelton (Oklahoma), Kathy Powers (Kansas), Susan Floyd and Stacie Glass (Missouri), Joyce Ray (Nevada). A special thanks goes to Oklahoma's Maddie Mahan, one of our newest rising stars who is also blessed with sharp eyed proofreading skills.

As I've said before, my greatest lessons have been taught to me by three divine muses, my daughters Persephone and Saskia and *corazon de mi corazon, mi querida*, Deidre.

Add reflections about your experience as a student.

The best teacher I ever had was Mrs. Carr .

If I wrote a letter to this great educator (and I should!) I'd say:

Thank you for caring about my reading skills. You gave me the confidence to read fluently out loud in front of my peers.

I had more than one boring instructor. If I wrote a mass email to them I'd say: It's not fun to learn all through lecture and note-taking. I don't like doing so as a teacher. Chance things up and be flexible.

What I can learn from my experience as a student that will guide me as an instructor is: To be a thoughtful, caring teacher because students today come from many different home lives. They need patience and caring in many ways.

CHAPTER 1

Whole Brain Teaching Overview

You cannot solve the problem with the same kind of thinking that created the problem.

— ALBERT EINSTEIN

Y ou've got a big choice.
Make it now.

You can choose to say that the problem in your classes is your students. They're out of control. They're disrespectful. They don't care about learning. Many teachers take this view and complain bitterly about their pupils.

If you believe the problem is with your kids, then close this book. There isn't anything either of us can do about your students. We can't visit their homes daily, get better jobs for their parents, retrain their siblings, turn off the electronic distractions, entice them to read, reward them for thinking critically. If you believe the problem is with your kids, Whole Brain Teaching is not for you.

A second choice is that your problem is how you teach your students. This is a wise choice because you've identified the teaching issue as something under your control. You can shape your character as an instructor by choosing effective teaching strategies. You can change you, by changing what you do in the classroom. Your students may be resistant learners, but they have no control over the tactics you employ to reform them.

Hopefully, you've made the second choice. The problem in teaching does not reside in kids, but in our teaching strategies. Every morning, we get up and look at the problem in the mirror.

Supported by cutting edge learning research, Whole Brain Teaching recognizes that students learn the most when they are engaged in lessons that involve seeing, hearing, doing, speaking, feeling and... laughing.

WBT unites two of the most vigorously researched, and applauded, teaching methods: direct interactive instruction (DII) and collaborative learning. By an odd, but understandable coincidence, more than one educator has described WBT as direct instruction on steroids. Our version of DII creates information packed lessons, amped up with good humor, that unfold with the tempo and engagement of a video game. In a Whole Brain classroom, every few minutes, pedagogical gears shift from DII to collaborative learning. No matter the vitality of our lessons, we know that the longer we talk, the more kids we lose. Brains, and not just young ones, stay sharply focused only for short periods. For us, student collaboration involves working in pairs, becoming happily energetic, Whole Brain teachers, paraphrasing and amplifying their instructor's lessons.

Available at WholeBrainTeaching.com, our K-12 modules include classroom management, lesson design, critical thinking, writing, reading and math. We are not a business. All our ebooks are free.

WBT techniques transform your students from passive receivers of information to dynamic creators of high-energy lessons.

What distinguishes Whole Brain Teaching from traditional education? We encourage students to be more active, not less. The traditional educator cries, "Quiet down! Knock it off! Pay attention!" The most fun kids have is when they're not learning. We exclaim, "More energy! Use giant gestures! Give me a Mighty Oh Yeah!" Whole Brain Teaching classrooms are learning dynamos powered by Funtricity. As soon as you enter a WBT class, you know you've left traditional education behind. The air is filled with task-focused laughter. The Golden Thread of Fun unites everything we do.

We believe the most effective classroom management is highly entertaining instruction. Want to reduce challenging behavior? Deliver fun-filled lessons. You are a successful WBT educator when your pupils are involved in every learning modality while grinning. Students love our lessons because we tickle their funny bones. The only merriment in traditional education is when kids happily escape from class.

Whole Brain Teaching: 122 Amazing Games! is packed with hilarious, powerful entertainments. Your kids will have so much fun, they won't notice how much they're learning. Inspired by conferences we've given to thousands of K-12 teachers across the country, WBT's games solve many classroom management problems as well as broaden your students' critical thinking skills, hone their writing ability, deepen their reading comprehension, develop their understanding of Common Core themes... all while activating their whole brains. Our contests will be marvelously effective no matter whether your pupils come to you from the inner city or grassy plains. One truth has delighted us over the last 15 years: it doesn't matter if students are English Language learners, Special Ed, gifted, wildly rambunctious or locked in their shells... the more brain areas activated in kids' classroom activities, the more they learn.

Think of the beginning of your journey as marked by large flags, the Big Seven. Our core instructional standards, hoisted by merry educators, wave above thousands of classrooms.

THE BIG SEVEN ~ Management Tools

1. **Class-Yes!** is WBT's infinitely variable, highly entertaining, attention getter.
2. **The Five Rules + A Diamond** address every classroom management problem, creating a dynamic, learning community.
   Rule 1: Follow directions quickly.
   Rule 2: Raise your hand for permission to speak.
   Rule 3: Raise your hand for permission to leave your seat.
   Rule 4: Make smart choices.
   Rule 5: Keep your dear teacher happy!
   ♦ **The Diamond Rule:** Keep your eyes on the target.

3. **Mirror Words** powerfully activates students' visual, auditory, and motor cortices, producing 100% engagement in your lessons.
4. **The Scoreboard** transforms classroom management into a living video game
5. **Teach-Okay** is our merry alternative to traditional education's dreary, think-pair-share.
6. **Hands and Eyes** alerts students that their dear teacher is about to make a Really Big Point.
7. **Switch** teaches chatty kids to listen carefully and quiet kids to speak boldly.

For a year-long teaching system and powerful techniques to re-form your most resistant learners, look at our education best seller, *Whole Brain Teaching for Challenging Kids* available on Amazon.com at http://goo.gl/NSLOQ.

Now, let's examine each Big Seven strategy, and then you'll be ready to explore 122 amazing, learning games.

CHAPTER 2

The Big Seven

You have brains in your head
And feet in your shoes.
You can steer yourself in any
Direction you choose.

— DR. SEUS

A t Whole Brain Teaching, we don't distinguish between classroom management and instructional delivery. We "manage" our classes by improving instruction; all our behavioral strategies involve powerful teaching techniques. We don't teach kids how to behave in one lesson and deliver academic instruction in the next. Engaging lessons that involve the whole brain are the most effective classroom management.

A popular behavioral technique in traditional education is the clippy chart. Every child's name is on a clothespin; moving pins up a color chart indicates positive behavior; moving pins down a color chart indicates negative behavior.

Here's the problem.

When a clothespin is moved, the instructor stops teaching to address the behavior of one student! Classroom management stops instruction!! In WBT, as you'll see, classroom management and lesson delivery are united; thinking well is behaving well. The techniques you use to teach your students our classroom rules are the same strategies you'll use to develop their reading, writing and math skills.

Here are our seven instructional tools, each one wrapped with good humor and field-tested by thousands of grinning instructors.

THE ATTENTION GETTER: Class-Yes!

When we want our students' attention, we say, "Class!" Our kids respond, "Yes!" If we say "Class! Class! Class!," students answer, "Yes! Yes! Yes!" Pupils of every age quickly learn, and happily respond, to this call-out and its variations. Before long, if you exclaim, "Class Bazinga!," your kids will exclaim "Yes Bazinga!" The more variety in your Attention Getter, the more engagement from your students.

THE STUDENT ENGAGER: Mirror Words

When we want 100% engagement in our classes (and when don't we?) a WBT instructor says, "Mirror words!" and holds up her hands. The students respond, "Mirror words!" and pick up their hands. The teacher speaks slowly and makes gestures illustrating the lesson. Her students repeat her words and mimic her gestures.

Mirroring gestures and repeating a lesson's words activates students' visual, motor and auditory cortices. Mirror lessons involve seeing, moving, hearing and speaking. *We don't have one exercise for kinesthetic learners, another exercise for visual learners, another exercise for auditory learners.* We address all learning styles simultaneously.

Imagine a basketball coach with dribbling drills for natural dribblers and shooting drills for natural shooters and rebounding drills for natural rebounders. The coach designs lessons for each player's strength, their natural ability, their learning style. Practices might be pleasant; every kid does what she does best. Of course, at game time, players flail whenever called on to perform outside their skill set.

The greatest athletes are often described as having "the whole package." They superbly perform every task involved in their sport. We want our students to be similarly blessed. In WBT, and specifically with Mirror Words, we don't focus on one learning style, but on all of a student's mental skills as an integrated whole. We want kids to develop every cognitive ability, not just their primary talents.

In Mirror Words we use two kinds of gestures, casual and memory. Casual gestures make lessons visual. If you are talking about active verbs, you might pump your arms as if you were running. If you are discussing the Mississippi, you might draw an invisible map in the air, tracing the river from Minnesota down to New Orleans. If you are talking about the Three Little Pigs, you might mime building houses of straw, sticks and bricks.

Memory gestures are motions that are linked to core concepts. If the lesson is on capital letters, you might raise one hand above the other showing a capital is a "big letter." If you were talking about sorting, you might pretend like you are dealing, sorting, cards. Predicting might be represented by thoughtfully scratching your head. Casual gestures can vary from teacher to teacher; memory gestures should be the same for every WBT educator in a school. Casual and memory gestures are powerfully communicated by Mirror Words.

Brain Fact:

There is no single memory area in the brain. Visual memories are stored in the visual cortex. Motor memories are stored in the motor cortex. Auditory memories are stored in the auditory cortex. The more brain areas involved in learning, as in Whole Brain Teaching, the more memories are created.

THE MOTIVATOR: The Scoreboard

In WBT we don't motivate students with candy, lottery tickets, play money, marbles in a jar or any of the trinkets sold online at Oriental Trading Company. We're teachers not carnival barkers. Giving away treats doesn't work... unless you want to turn kids into beggars.

Dear Colleagues. Throw away the Treasure Chest!!!
In place of junk, we use a T diagram.

Here are a collection of grade level Scoreboards, starting with kindergarten.

Level I

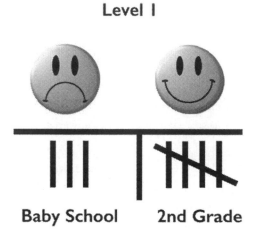

Baby School   **2nd Grade**

To motivate with academics, rather than candy, we label the positive side of the Scoreboard two grade levels higher than the current grade. In kindergarten, the negative side is Baby School; avoiding babyhood is a powerful motivator for five year olds.

Here's a third grade Scoreboard.

Level I

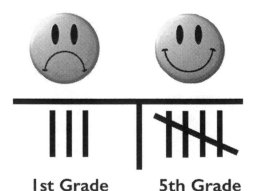

I st Grade   **5th Grade**

In upper grades, we label the negative side two grade levels lower; thus the Frowny side for third grade would be first grade.

In secondary, where students are not keen on Smiley and Frowny faces, we use these alternatives (samples are for high school freshmen).

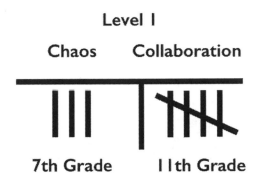

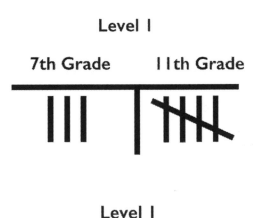

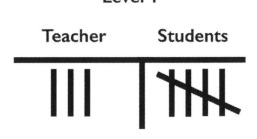

Detailed information about WBT in middle school and high school is found in "Power Teaching for Challenging Teens" and "Industrial

Strength Whole Brain Teaching," available under "Free Ebooks" at WholeBrainTeaching.com.

One side of the Scoreboard charts positive behavior and the other side charts negative behavior. When the class receives a positive mark, they clap their hands and exclaim "Oh yeah!" Examples of positive behavior include: quickly lining up or sitting down, moving to the carpet with minimum chaos, using large gestures when teaching a neighbor, consistently raising hands for permission to speak, listening intently to the teacher's directions, etc.

In third grade, when we record a Smiley mark on the fifth grade side, we make statements like, "That's the way fifth graders focus on solving a math problem!... Oh goodness, that was fifth grade speed in preparing for your essay!... The whole back row is reading this difficult passage as intensely as fifth graders!"

When students receive a negative mark on the Scoreboard, they lift their shoulders and groan, "Oh!" Examples of negative behavior are, as you might expect, the opposite of positive behavior, lining up or sitting down slowly, taking forever to prepare study materials, spacing out while the teacher talks, etc.

The class as a whole can receive a positive mark on the Scoreboard for the outstanding behavior of one student. We love shining the spotlight on our model kids or on students who, out of the blue, produce positive actions. *However, we never give the class a mark for the negative actions of one pupil.* Some students, often our most challenging, revel in the attention of costing everyone a Frowny. When several kids speak without raising their hands, a negative mark might be made on the Scoreboard. However, when Maria blurts out, even repeatedly, she doesn't cost the class a Frowny.

The difference between positive and negative marks should never be greater than three; if you reward students too often, they become lackadaisical; if you punish too frequently, they become aggravated. Keep the Scoreboard game excitingly close.

Note that we have headlined the Scoreboard with Level 1. For a generation raised with video games, this makes our motivator irresistibly engaging. When kids ask, "What do we get for winning?"

You reply, "Win enough times and, just like a video game, you move up a level!"

In the next chapter, we'll describe the Scoreboard levels, which, remarkably enough, are the same from kindergarten through high school.

THE CLASS UNIFIER: The Five Classroom Rules + A Diamond

In the first weeks of school, teach your students the Five Classroom Rules and The Diamond.

Rule 1: Follow directions quickly.
Rule 2: Raise your hand for permission to speak.
Rule 3: Raise your hand for permission to leave your seat.
Rule 4: Make smart choices.
Rule 5: Keep your dear teacher happy!
♦ **The Diamond Rule:** Keep your eyes on the target.

In this section, we'll describe each rule and then provide a simple, two step plan, for implementation.

Rule 1: Follow directions quickly.

The secret to lightening fast, classroom transitions.

Please don't read this, unless you have medical clearance. Be sure your doctor guarantees that your ticker can take the thrill of watching your class zip, with lightening speed, from one activity to another.

Twenty years ago in Yucaipa, California, when we were designing the fundamentals of Whole Brain Teaching, we had no problem agreeing that Rule 1, for classroom management, should be "Follow directions quickly!" Slow transitions from reading to writing to math to lining up, at every grade, not only wasted time but also were breeding grounds for disruptive activity. If, for some nightmarish reason, you wanted an out of control classroom, encourage slow, lazy transitions and before long... your kids will be bouncing off the walls.

Ponder these truths. Our students open their books slowly because we never take time to teach them to open their books quickly. Kids, of every age, take forever to get out a piece of paper because we have never taught them to do this rapidly. Children, day after day, week after week, line up in wacky fashion because the only time we teach them how to line up is when they are actually lining up... which is precisely when we have no time to teach anything!

Here is a simple, two step procedure, classroom tested by tens of thousands of teachers, for helping your kids to follow directions quickly.

Step One

After teaching your students Rule 1 in the first minutes of your class, vigorously rehearse the rule, five times a day. You say, "Rule 1" and hold up one finger. Your students say, "Follow directions quickly!" and rapidly swim one hand through the air, like a fish darting downstream. Do not go to Step Two until your kids instantly respond, merrily respond!, to your Rule 1 cue. The more entertaining you make this rehearsal, the more engaged your students will be in following the rule. One of our mottos at WBT is *students learn the most when they are having the most fun learning.*

Step Two

Teach your kids the Three-Peat. You say, "Yellow folders out!" They say, "Yellow folders out! Yellow folders out! Yellow folders out!" as they pull out their yellow folders. When the folder is open to the correct page, we suggest kids shoot both hands upward, waggle their fingers, and happily murmur, "Yea!" They continue their celebration, until the teacher sweeps a hand dramatically through the air. You can use the celebration time to help students who are slow.

Using the Three-Peat, if you say, "pencils ready!," your kids exclaim, "Pencils ready! Pencils ready! Pencils ready!" and wiggle their pencils in celebration, until you signal it is time for silence.

Listen to me my dear colleague! Don't try to teach lining up right before the bell rings. You don't have time. Rehearse lining up five times a day, when you are not fighting the clock. You say, "Lines!" Your kids exclaim, "Lines! Lines, Lines!" and line up according to the pattern you have established. You say "Seats!" and they exclaim, "Seats! Seats! Seats!," celebrating when they are sitting down. For extra motivation, time these activities with a stopwatch. Then, as you gasp in delight, watch as your kids race to set new, transition records.

The more you rehearse any procedure, and the more entertaining you make the rehearsal, the quicker your students will perform a classroom transition.

Please calm down. A rapidly beating heart is a sure sign you are approaching Teacher Heaven.

The transitions I need to work on are: _____

_____

_____

*My plan is to:*_____

_____

_____

Rule 2: Raise your hand for permission to speak.

Rule 3: Raise your hand for permission to leave your seat.

Taming Blurters and Wanderers

In the middle of your Civil War lesson, a chatty kid blurts out, "What time is lunch?!" You blurt back, "How many times do I have to tell you to raise your hand to speak! Raise your hand! Raise your hand!" You match your student's emotional blurting, with your own.

Welcome to Teaching Purgatory. Too often, we treat students like we don't want to be treated. Chained together for a year, we mirror their outbursts with our own. We try to put out a kid's little flame, with our big fire.

Why do children (and teachers) blurt? In scientific terms, there are more connections from the brain's limbic system to the pre-frontal cortex than vice versa. Translation: emotions control reason more easily than reason controls emotions. Another scientific point: our brain's mirror neurons condition us to imitate behavior we observe. You blurt me. I blurt you. And so on. Hear those people yelling at each other over there? It's Teaching Purgatory's merry-go-round.

Scolding doesn't change behavior. If chastising a child transformed them into a model student, I'd write best sellers, "Scold Like a Pro!," "The Five Secrets of Power Chastisement," "If They're Not Crying, They Didn't Get It: Confessions of a Former Sweetie Pie."

If scolding doesn't change behavior, what does? Practice. You have your choice between two tennis coaches. One coach scolds you for your bad technique. The other coach helps you practice good strokes. Which one will improve your game? Don't know what to do with an unruly student or class? Practice good behavior.

Here's Whole Brain Teaching's two-step procedure, classroom tested for a decade across the U.S., for transforming Blurters into Hand Raisers (as a footnote, I'll describe how the same strategy works with kids who wander the classroom without permission).

Step One

By the end of the first week or two of school, you should be reviewing classroom rules five times a day. For Whole Brain Teaching's Rule 2, hold up two fingers and say, "Rule 2!" Your kids respond, "Raise your hand for permission to speak." They shoot one hand into the air and then quickly bring it down beside their mouth, making talking motions with their fingers. Make this rehearsal fun. Use a variety of intonations and deliveries. Fun imitates fun. Keep everyone's mirror neurons happy.

Step Two

By the end of week three, most of your pupils will have Rule 2 down pat. Then, say, "You're doing pretty good with Rule 2, but now let's see how you are at helping your classroom friends follow the rule. I'm going to pretend as if I'm talking. Renaldo, you interrupt me without raising your hand and say, 'I have a new puppy." (Renaldo is one of your brightest, boldest kids.)

Speak a few words about any subject and nod at Renaldo. He interrupts you, "I have a new puppy!" Congratulate him. Great blurting!

Then continue, "Class, let's do that again. But this time when Renaldo interrupts me, I'll say Rule 2 and you exclaim, making the hand motion, 'Raise your hand for permission to speak!'"

You talk. Renaldo starts to blurt. Immediately interrupt him and call for Rule 2. Your kids respond in a flash, "Raise your hand for permission to speak!" Their limbic systems delight in shutting down a classmate's limbic system.

We call this approach Wrong Way-Right Way. Practice the Wrong Way. Then, practice the Right Way. Over and over. You're building reason's strength to rein in frisky, student emotions.

Use the same approach for Whole Brain Teaching's Rule 3, "Raise your hand for permission to leave your seat." Rehearse the rule with the hand gesture, students raise their hands, then walk their fingers through the air. Then, use Wrong Way-Right Way.

Reynaldo, on your cue, leaves his seat without permission. Great job of breaking the rule. Reynaldo leaves his seat again, you call out Rule 3, and the kids exclaim, "Raise your hand for permission to leave your seat!"

If you practice the wrong way and then right way, five times a day, pretty soon you'll see more right way behavior. *No student ever wants to feel like they are doing something wrong...* that's why they deny they're engaged in incorrect behavior.

"Maggie, stop doing that!"

"I wasn't doing anything!"

This is the wonder. With the procedures described above, you take a classroom disruption, blurting or wandering, and transform it into a classroom unifier. Whenever a rule is broken, a rule is strengthened.

That's the way it is, my friends, in Teaching Heaven.

Rule 4: Make smart choices.

The Ancient Secret for Wise Decisions

Let's think about the first three Whole Brain Teaching classroom rules. Each will help solve one teaching problem. Implementing Rule 1, "Follow directions quickly," will speed classroom transitions. Implementing Rule 2, "Raise your hand for permission to speak," will produce orderly discussions. Implementing Rule 3, "Raise your hand for permission to leave you seat" will keep your classroom from turning into kiddie bumper cars.

Rule 4 "Make smart choices" is a much larger, grander principle.

Making smart choices is perhaps the fundamental rule for all human activities, in or out of the classroom. As I can testify after teaching philosophy for four decades, philosophers from Socrates in 5th century B.C. Athens to Jean Paul Sartre in 20th century Paris disagreed about almost everything, except one guiding idea: Humans should use their reason carefully... they should make smart choices.

Socrates believed smart choices involved self-knowledge; Plato argued that the smartest choice was to study mathematics in order to contemplate eternal truths; Sartre held that the smartest choice was living authentically, never blaming others for your life situation. Despite their disagreements, philosophers have believed the good life was found through exercising our reason in wise decision making.

Whole Brain Teachers have discovered that Rule 4 is wonderfully powerful. The rule covers every area of a student's life at school, at home, out with friends, on the Internet, engaged in a sport or hobby, Everything. From childhood to adulthood, we need to make smart choices. Rule 4 is especially powerful in covering every kind of disruptive student behavior, in or out of class.

Happily enough, implementing the Smart Choices rule is easy.

Step One

Review the classroom rules five times a day. Teach your pupils that the gesture for Rule 4, "Make smart choices" is tapping their temple with their forefinger, three times. At random moments during the day, call out "Rule 4" (or any of the other rules). Your students should instantly respond with the rule itself and its accompanying gesture.

Step Two

After your pupils have mastered Rule 4, "Make smart choices" and the gesture, your only problem will be to choose from a host of opportunities for implementation. Discuss the smart and foolish choices made by characters in a story, famous people in a history lesson, kids in the lunchroom, athletes in a game. Before beginning a calendar exercise or art activity, ask kids to talk about the smart and foolish decisions they could make.

Here's a key point. If a child claims, incorrectly in your view, that one of her choices was smart, you respond, "Okay. But what would be a smarter choice?" This may involve considerable discussion, but it is worthwhile. Teach your pupils that smarter choices are always possible.

Rule 4 on the playground

We've presented Whole Brain Teaching techniques to countless educators at conferences and never talked about how Rule 4 could be applied to the playground. Shame on us!

Try saying something like this to your class (with techniques like

Mirror Words and Teach-Okay, of course). "We're going to talk about Rule 4, making smart choices, on the playground. To make this fun and clear, we'll use two finger action figures. Using two fingers on each hand, walk your action figures around on your desk. (Kids do so.) Good! Now, imagine your desk is the playground. Pretend as if your two finger action figures are making foolish choices while playing tetherball. Show your neighbor what that would look like and explain what each action figure would say. (Kids, laughing, do so.) Good! Now, show your neighbor, using smart two finger action figures, what smart choices playing tether ball would look and sound like."

Virtually every wacky behavior that goes on during recess can be acted out, and corrected, with foolish and smart two finger action figures... and nothing gets scraped except imaginary knees.

Let's say, Junie comes up to you during recess, very upset about what happened to her on the slide. To lower Junie's emotional temperature, ask her to show you, using two finger action figures, Martin's foolish choices and how she reacted. Then, using your action figures, show Junie the smartest choices available to her, should a similar situation arise. Finally, if necessary, take yourself over to Martin to see if your action figures can teach his action figures to follow Rule 4.

Rule 5: Keep your dear teacher happy!

Need a rule that stops back talking students in their tracks? Discover the golden signpost on the road to Teaching Heaven.

When we began to develop Whole Brain Teaching's rules, our goal was to cover every classroom problem.

We wanted a couple of principles that were as specific as possible and one or two others that covered every variety of disruptive behavior.

Thus, we have three rules that target individual classroom problems.

As described previously, we use Rule 1: "Follow directions quickly" to address slow transitions.

Rule 2: "Raise your hand for permission to speak," targets kids who are spontaneously chatty.

Rule 3: "Raise your hand for permission to leave your seat," keeps students seated during instruction.

Unfortunately, these three rules don't cover every classroom misbehavior. Rule 4 "Make smart choices" is marvelously general, addressing every decision a child can make. Rule 4 can be applied to any issue not covered by the first three rules.

So, why do we need Rule 5, "Keep your dear teacher happy?" Rule 5 addresses your most challenging students... *the ones who will quarrel with you about Rules 1-4!*

Pupils who dawdle along, can claim they are following directions quickly.

Chatty kids can claim they weren't speaking to anyone.

Your most challenging students can even deny they are out of their seat... when they are standing in the middle of the classroom! "I'm not out of my seat. I'm just getting my pencil sharpened."

Of course, your most resistant spirits can argue that all their choices are smart, no matter how obviously foolish.

So, what's a beleaguered instructor to do? *You need one rule that can't be disputed.* We've never discovered a child who could convince their instructor that their disruptive behavior made the teacher happy! Rule 5 is the argument stopper, the backtalk squelcher.

If a parent or administrator is troubled by the rule, explain, "I know Rule 5, 'Keep your dear teacher happy' sounds like it is about me, but that's not the case. My only happiness is seeing my students learn."

Here's a two-step procedure to implement Rule 5.

Step One

As mentioned above, for a minute or so, five times a day, rehearse the five classroom rules. You call the rule number; your pupils rapidly reply with the rule and matching gesture. After three to four weeks, place special emphasis on Rule 5. During rehearsals and at random times during the day, call "Rule 5!" Students respond, "Keep your dear teacher happy!" while framing their smiling faces with their fingers.

As an explanation of the rule, say something like the following to your class, "It doesn't take presents, or anything you can buy, to keep me happy. I only want one thing, one thing in the whole wide world, and that's seeing you learn. Your growth as students fills my heart with joy."

Step Two

Once students can instantly respond with the rule and gesture, when you exclaim "Rule 5," you're ready for implementation.

Pick a lively student, Sarah, and say, "I'm going to pretend like I'm teaching and then I'll say to you, 'Sarah please pay attention.' I want you to respond, with real attitude, 'I am paying attention!'" Model for Sarah, several times, how she should reply. This will be wonderfully shocking to your class... a student gets to backtalk you! And so, the little skit is played. When Sarah talks back, you exclaim, "Great job Sarah! That was a wonderful example of breaking Rule 5! Class, give her a Ten Finger Woo!!" Your kids extend their wiggling fingers toward Sarah and exclaim, "Woo!" (More fun than applause.)

Then say, "This time when Sarah backtalks, I'll say 'Rule 5'. I want you to respond using our gesture and quickly say, 'Keep your dear teacher happy!'"

Follow this routine once or twice until the class instantly implements the Rule 5 response.

For several days, and whenever necessary thereafter, practice a routine like the one just described. We've found that the key to stopping challenging behavior is to practice the class response, before disruption occurs.

The only problem we've discovered with implementing Rule 5 is that students employ it too eagerly! Your dear kids will start calling out "Rule 5!" whenever they hear the slightest guff. When this occurs say, with a broad, honest grin, "I appreciate how quickly you are using Rule 5... but believe me, I will let you know when I think it's necessary." *Oh happy day... your kids have your back at the faintest whisper of ornery behavior!!!*

The Diamond Rule: Keep your eyes on the target.

The Diamond Rule is a recent addition to Whole Brain Teaching's instructional jewels. Chris Rekstad, co-founder of WBT, told me he had a truly remarkable collection of challenging kids. Poor me, I didn't believe him and went to see for myself. Oh my friends! Even when I had my teaching engine fired up to its highest power, I kept thinking, "half these kids aren't even looking at me!" Then, I thought how often, especially in the afternoon at my conferences, a large handful of instructors found other objects of attention besides their dear teacher.

Instruction begins, and is maintained, by students looking in the right direction. The target could be the teacher, the board, their book, another student, a video, a science experiment. Your kids won't learn much if they aren't looking where they should be looking.

The gesture for the Diamond Rule, "Keep your eyes on the target" is pointing two fingers at your eyes, then pointing two fingers at yourself (or the current target). You can introduce the Diamond Rule in the first minute of the first day or save it until later in the term. Like a miser, you'll delight in the beauty of this pedagogical jewel.

Step One

As with the other rules, frequently teach and rehearse the Diamond Rule and its gesture. Then, even in the middle of lecture, when you exclaim, "Diamond!," your kids will respond, "Keep your eyes on the target." Their gesture should be, two fingers from their eyes to whatever is the current target, you, another student, their books, whatever.

Step Two

Whenever necessary, use Wrong Way/Right Way practice to reinforce the Diamond Rule. Tell your kids to act like whatever grade is on the negative side of the Scoreboard. You talk, they glance around the room. Oh, what a fascinating ceiling. Have Maria, a good kid, stand and address the class, while she is bluntly ignored by her peers. Being ignored deeply hurts. Then, ask one of your challenging kids to stand up, speak, and suffer while classmates look around the room.

Next, as always, start Right Way practice. "Show me how students two grades higher, very grown up, would behave when someone is teaching." Happily enough, students love to imitate mature behavior. The last thing kids want is to be kids. You talk and suddenly your third graders are staring at you with their version of fifth grade intensity.

Brain Fact:

There are more connections from the brain's limbic system (emotions) to the prefrontal cortex (reason), than the other way around. Emotions control our reason more easily than reason controls emotions. The more you scold your students, the more likely you are to receive emotional, rather than a rational, responses.

THE ACTIVATOR: Teach-Okay

The longer you talk, the more kids you lose. As a powerful corrective to lecturing, speak briefly, no more than 2-4 sentences at a time. Then, give kids the opportunity to rehearse your lesson with each other. (In kindergarten, WBT teachers work up to Teach-Okay, with "tell your neighbor.")

SCRIPT: TEACH-OKAY (Third Grade)

Teacher: Class! Class!

Students: Yes! Yes!

Teacher: Mirror words!

Students: Mirror words!

Teacher: (Holding one fist above the other) A fraction has two numbers.

Students: (Mirroring the teacher's gestures) A fraction has two numbers.

Teacher: (waggling the top fist) The top number is the numerator.

Students: (Mirroring the teacher's gesture) The top number is the numerator.

Teacher: (waggling the bottom fist) The bottom number is the denominator.

Students: (Mirroring the teacher's gestures) The bottom number is the denominator.

Teacher: Now, make a full turn to your neighbors, use giant gestures and explain the numerator and denominator. (claps twice) Teach!

Students: (Clapping twice) Okay! (Students teach their neighbors about the numerator and denominator.)

Teach-Okay is WBT's answer to traditional education's weary think-pair-share. You may be concerned that we don't give students time to contemplate the teacher's point. We believe that when we ask kids to "think," we have no way to tell what they're thinking about. Is it what we just said or how to get to the head of the lunch line? Talking through a response is a good way to think through a response. Call it "ideational fluency." Students hear a teacher's point and immediately start paraphrasing it to a neighbor.

Video examples of the Teach-Okay are in the Resources section on page 75.

THE INVOLVER: Switch!

We want our chatty students to learn to listen attentively and our quiet students to learn to speak boldly. When kids use the Teach-Okay, they take turns. One student is the speaker; the other is the listener. The speaker repeats the lesson and makes gestures; the listener mimics the speaker's gestures. When the speaker is finished, the students exchange a high five and say, "Switch!" The speaker becomes the listener and the listener becomes the speaker. For example, Lawana is the speaker and explains, using gestures, a lesson on the rain forest to Tim. Tim mirrors Lawana's gestures, and if he wishes, repeats her words. Lawana finishes, gives Tim a high five, and both students say, "Switch!" Tim becomes the speaker and Lawana the listener. Students continue exchanging roles until the teacher calls, "Class!"

THE FOCUSER: Hands and Eyes

Occasionally, maybe once every five to ten minutes, you have a large point that requires your students' intense attention. With a loud, firm voice say, "Hands and eyes!" Quickly fold your hands. Your kids reply, "Hands and eyes!" and quickly fold their hands. State your large point, delighting in the focused stares of your class. For especially important announcements, exclaim, "Hands! Hands! Hands and eyes!," clapping your hands together. Your kids repeat what you said and wait, breathlessly, for your next words.

In the games that follow, we'll often mention one, or more, of the Big Seven. Let's start with our Top Ten Games... our most irresistible entertainments.

(Begin these games at any point of the year. If you're starting late in the term, simply say, "Usually about this time of the semester, I move to a more advanced system. I think you kids are ready.")

CHAPTER 3

Top 10 Games

The playing child advances forward to
new stages of mastery.

— ERIK H. ERIKSON

Eight of our top 10 games focus on classroom management. You'll discover teacher tested entertainments that improve behavior, nourish individual growth, increase motivation, develop leadership, and strategies that reform challenging kids, Beloved Rascals. In addition, you'll explore a powerful game for developing writing skills and an irresistible, core knowledge review contest.

Let's begin with an overview.

1. **Super Improvers:** perhaps our most powerful game; reward students for improvement, not ability.
2. **The Brainy Game:** A cartoon collection of gestures that simplifies instruction in critical thinking and writing.
3. **The Scoreboard:** A yearlong motivation system that transforms your classroom into a living video game.
4. **Leaders Rule:** Kindergarten to high school, you need a method for training student leaders, our most underutilized education resource.
5. **Practice Cards:** Explore our counter-intuitive approach to reforming Beloved Rascals, giving them fewer, not more, choices.
6. **Short Talk, Long Talk, Plan Together:** Discover the best way to structure one on one interchanges with disruptive students.

7. **Wrong Way/Right Way Practice:** What to do, when you don't know what to do.
8. **Mind Soccer:** Dream of a game that kids beg to play... they work incredibly hard to earn the privilege of playing... and all the contest involves is a review everything you've taught.
9. **Classroom Engagement Average:** Classes improve at the pace of a glacier. You need a simple system to tell if you're getting anywhere.
10. **Challenging Kid Average:** Chart growth, not frustration!

1. SUPER IMPROVERS

Our primary goal in Whole Brain Teaching is to reward students for improvement, rather than ability. We praise better work more often than excellent work. In traditional education, rewards for ability result in the same students winning recognition, year after year. Too often our most gifted kids skate by with minimum effort while less talented students bail out of a race the system has taught them they can't win.

When you reward for improvement, every student receives positive attention for breaking personal records. Special Ed and gifted pupils find themselves in a lively competition on the same playing field. Maria's parents never graduated from elementary school; Herman's parents are both doctors. Both students increase their reading speed by 10%. In a traditional classroom, Maria, a weak reader, might fail while Herman gets Student of the Week. In a Whole Brain classroom, equal rewards (as you will see) are bestowed on Maria and Herman. We celebrate growth, more than skill. Herman has to keep pushing hard, day after day, or watch as Maria wins recognition as a Super Improver. The message we communicate to our kids, over and over, is that the only person you have to surpass is yourself. Our mantra, once more, *reward for improvement not ability*. Our fundamental strategy is the Super Improver Team.

> **Super Improvers Online**
>
> Webcast 503, 563
> http://goo.gl/j2YPx4
> http://goo.gl/c1n1JO
> http://goo.gl/iqCyqf
>
> WBT YouTube
> http://goo.gl/8jbLlm

Super Improver Team: Elementary

Living Legend	Student 1	Student 2	Student 3
Hall of Fame	Student 4	Student 5	Student 6
Super Star	Student 7	Student 8	Student 9
MVP	Student 10	Student 11	Student 12
Star	Student 13	Student 14	Student 15
Captain	Student 16	Student 17	Student 18
Leader			
Starter	Student 19	Student 20	Student 21
Rookie			
Fan	Student 22	Student 23	Student 24

Post the Super Improvers Team display on a wall as early as the first day or as late as the third week. The Scoreboard's focus, as you'll see later, is the class as a whole; the Super Improvers Team's focus is the individual.

Create a 10 level, color coded scale; create names for each level, ascending from least, to most, exciting. A nature theme might begin with snail and climb up to falcon. An ocean theme might begin with plankton and ascend to blue whale. Put every student's name (or number) on the right side of the display.

On the first day of the Super Improvers Team, set one or two goals for all students. For example, every pupil can improve in following Rule 1 and writing neatness (or, increasing reading speed, use of gestures when teaching a neighbor, mastery of math facts, etc.). When you see improvement, praise the student. If the pattern continues for several days, award a star. After 10 stars, the kid's color changes. For example, you've decided to focus on rewarding for Rule 1 improvement, "Follow directions quickly." Hector, a bit of a slowpoke, shows increases in speed when getting out his study materials. Praise him. If he continues for a few days, becoming the new Speedy Hector, give him a Super Improver star on his name. Daphne, naturally quick, peps it up even more than normal when cleaning up her desk. Praise her new talents for several days. Then, give Daphne her star.

Our yearlong strategy begins with lots of praise at the start of the year and few stars. This makes improvement stars valuable. Mid-year, less praise and more stars. In the spring, when you really need student energy, it's raining stars!

Now, please pay close attention. *You have to change your goggles. You're not looking for the good kids. You're looking for improving kids. You cannot pick an improvement goal for the whole class, unless everyone can show growth in reaching that goal.* Therefore, don't use quietly walking in the hall as a class target, unless every student makes a ruckus when they leave the room. A common mistake that educators make with the Super Improvers team is rewarding good, rather than improved, behavior. "Look at how nicely Melvin writes, class! He gets a Super Improver star!" No star for Melvin unless his neat handwriting becomes even neater. Ida's handwriting is illegible; she has many virtues, but writing clearly isn't one of them. But look here! Ida found a way to write more neatly! Give that girl praise... day after day. Then, award Ida a star for her new handwriting skill.

Change class goals whenever you wish, but for students to show growth (and to focus on how they can improve) you should keep targets for about a week. We suggest a maximum of two weekly goals, one academic and one social.

Academic targets for the class could include increasing reading speed, mastering math facts, improving handwriting, increased essay complexity, improved assessment scores, amped up energy in teaching classmates, expanded use of vocabulary words, etc.

Class social targets could include increased kindness, praise of classmates, use of language identified as "good manners," selfless behavior, good sportsmanship, considerate leadership, mentoring lower grade students. Positive social skills are more difficult for students to identify than improvement in test scores. Thus, it's best to give clear targets. "This week, I am looking for improvement in our manners. Today I just want to hear you say 'please' more often. Tomorrow, we will add 'thank you.'" Or, "I've never seen anyone in this class play with Mrs. Johnson's students. I'd love to see improvement in that area." (Mrs. Johnson's students are Special Ed.) Or, "I see a lot of litter on the playground and I haven't seen anyone from our class picking it up. Gosh, I wonder if we could improve in keeping our school cleaner?" Or, "We all need to improve on Rule 1. Let's pick up the pace... all day!!" Or, "We have a wonderful custodian, a great bus driver, and marvelous women in the lunch room. I want to see my kids smiling at these wonderful people and saying 'hi!'" Or, "When I ask you to do something, I'd be happy to hear one lovely word, 'Okay!' It would be even more thrilling to hear, "Okay, Mr. Biffle!'"

After several weeks, give a small group of students individual goals. Juan needs to work on keeping his hands to himself. Martina should read more upper grade books. Change class and individual goals as necessary but don't have too many individual targets because this creates a bookkeeping nightmare. For your most challenging kids, set improvement goals that will be the easiest for them to reach. Privately, tell Murry, "If you could keep your feet off the desk before first recess, that would be an improvement."

Your natural tendency with challenging kids is to ask them to improve their most aggravating behavior. But this is not immediately possible. Sammy's crying is aggravating because it is so frequent. It's so frequent because his outbursts are a natural reaction to a frustrating world... a natural reaction that is deeply wired into his brain's dendrites. *Give your challenging kids improvement goals that are easiest for them to achieve.* If you tell Sammy that his one goal is to stop crying, then he'll learn, before long, that an improvement star is out of his reach.

A strategy we've found effective with our Beloved Rascals is to give them a list of behaviors and let them choose which one they think would be the simplest for them to improve. For students who have a difficult time with self control, set up the list so the behaviors are isolated to a time period: keeping your hands to yourself in line before first recess, keeping your hands to yourself when walking to the library in the afternoon, etc. You could include crying on Sammy's list, but within time periods or parameters: no crying if you lose at tether ball, no crying about crayons during morning drawing.

To sum up: reward for improvement not ability. Reward for better behavior, not excellent behavior. Choose one or two class goals, academic and social, and keep these for about a week. Pick 3-5 students, gifted, rambunctious, troubled, for individual improvement goals. For your most challenging kids, select simple, well defined, targets. Reward improvement with stars on the student's name. When the pupil earns 10 stars, she moves up a level. Thus, if the bottom level is white and the next level is blue, Maria moves up from white to blue after her tenth star at the white level.

Consider integrating video game features into your Super Improvers Team. The success of video games among our youth is no accident. Game designers, over the last three decades, have hit upon a handful of incredibly pleasure producing strategies. Research at Stanford indicates that playing video games increases the brain's production of dopamine, the neurotransmitter associated with the strongest feelings of pleasure.

One of the most common features of video games is that the player advances up levels. I don't know why this feature is so intoxicating... but consumers spend billions of dollars for the opportunity to achieve imaginary victories in a pixel world. In WBT, we've never found a student who can resist the thrill of moving up levels on the Super Improver Team, or a class that is not motivated by climbing toward higher regions of the Scoreboard. The more you emphasize the thrill of moving up levels in either of these WBT games, the more learning engagement you'll create.

You may not be video game literate, but your kids, especially your challenging boys, have the equivalent of electronic game doctorates.

Power-ups are a common feature of video games. When you successfully move up a level, you are awarded a new, sometimes temporary, power, a key that unlocks a secret, a bomb that destroys trolls, a cloak of invisibility. We want the Super Improvers Team to develop leaders and so, moving up levels awards students with increased leadership powers.

Here is a power up schedule you might explore. Classroom leaders are Call Outers. When you point at them, they call out a WBT classroom strategy: Class!, Mirror Words, Hands and Eyes, Teach!, Rule 1, 2, 3, 4, 5, demo of Mighty Oh Yeah or Mighty Groan, Class-boom, Switch, Silent Mirror, Magic Mirror. Every morning, write the call out strategies on the board. Start with Class! and then, as the year unfolds, make the list longer. The higher a player is on the Super Improver Team, the more frequently you will point at him or her for the call out. You hope that students on lower levels complain that they are rarely selected. Wonderful! Say, "Show more improvement, climb higher on the Super Improver wall, and you will be a Call Outer with many opportunities to exercise your leadership powers!!!"

Another common feature, especially in adventure video games, is role-playing. As needed to enrich your students' engagement, use the following roles:

Secret Improver: when you write SI beside students' names they are a Secret Improver. Privately, give them individual goals that will earn them stars. This is a powerful strategy for your most challenging kids. As described earlier, give these students targets that are simple to hit. Keep the Secret Improver group small or the record keeping will become too complex.

Ninja Spy: when you write NS beside students' names they are Ninja Spies. Their job is to secretly observe positive behavior and slip a note into the Ninja Spy Box describing who did what. Occasionally, read the notes to your class. Wow! I wonder who those Ninja Spies will notice next??

Rovers: when you write R beside students' names they are Rovers. At your request, Rovers wander the classroom helping their classmates.

Mysterion: add the name of Mysterion to the Super Improvers Team. Occasionally, Mysterion gets a star. Who is Mysterion, everyone wonders? When the suspense is extreme, reveal the secret identity. You're Mysterion working on your own teaching improvements!

For secondary students, create a Super Improvers League that includes all your classes.

Super Improver Team: Secondary

	Period 1 ☆☆
Living Legend	Student 1, 2, 3, 4, 5
Hall of Fame	Period 2 ☆☆☆
Super Star	Student 1, 2, 3, 4, 5 ☆
MVP	Period 3 ☆☆
Star	Student 1, 2, 3, 4, 5
Captain	Period 4 ☆☆☆
Leader	Student 1, 2, 3, 4, 5
Starter	Period 5
Rookie	Student 1, 2, 3, 4, 5
Fan	Period 6 ★★★
	Student 1, 2, 3, 4, 5

As always, reward for improvement, not ability. Because you don't see your kids as often as students in elementary school, five, not ten, stars moves a class up a level. Begin with start of the year goals. "If 50% of the class can be in their seat before the tardy bell, your period will get a star." Courtesy of Sarah Meador, middle school instructor and WBT Executive Board member, here is a schedule of improvements. Substitute your own as needed.

- 60% of students in seats before bell rings
- Raise to 75%
- Raise to 85%
- Raise to 95%
- Add, homework completed by 50%
- Homework completed by 75%
- Homework completed by 85%
- Add, energetically reviewing course material before the teacher begins to lecture.
- Add, consistently using full turn during Teach-Okay
- Add, consistently using large gestures during Teach-Okay
- Substitute for any of the above, a class percentage on the next test. "If the class average on Friday's exam is 75%, the class gets a star and beats Period 2!"

Use the leadership training system, described on page 56, to identify class leaders. Place leaders' names beside each period. As they improve in classroom behavior and/or academics, leaders earn a star for their class. When you have teen leaders buy in, and they will, you've entered Upper Grade Instructional Paradise.

Ultimate Super Improvers: Many games in this book feature students setting and breaking personal records. Some of the most popular are *SuperSpeed 100, SuperSpeed 1000, SuperSpeed Math* and *Genius Ladder.* Popular educational software like *Accelerated Reader* are also designed to recognize individual improvement. With some experimenting, you'll discover that the Super Improver system is flexible enough that you could award stars for a host of classroom activities.

Our second game, one of our newest and most popular entertainments, will powerfully develop your students' critical thinking and writing skills.

2. THE BRAINY GAME

Brainies are images of gestures, each one representing a key critical thinking or writing concept. You'll find a detailed description of this brain based, teaching system in *The Brainy Game*, a 200 page eBook at WholeBrainTeaching.com, under "Free Ebooks/general."

Brainies Online

Webcast 574, 579, 589,
http://goo.gl/NDeZYJ
http://goo.gl/96Jx9w
http://goo.gl/oJlfjy

WBT YouTube
http://goo.gl/ThqyGO
http://goo.gl/xlpfWg
http://goo.gl/qCBnVC

Here's the Brainy collection, a complete K-12 critical thinking/writing system on two pages!

Download *The Brainy Game* and give each student a laminated, two sided, copy of the images on the next page. One side lists the gestures and terms; the other side only shows the gestures. Thus, for ease of quizzing and review, you've created the world's largest flash card.

Pick the Brainies you want your kids to learn. In kindergarten, students can master about 15-20 in a year. First to third graders can often learn most of the Brainies by Christmas break. Older students can master the Brainies in a few weeks.

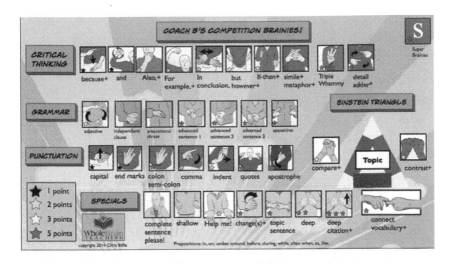

The Brainies represent a host of key concepts.

Critical Thinking: because, and, also, for example, in conclusion, but, however, if-then, simile-metaphor, Triple Whammy (see below), detail adder

Grammar: adjective, independent clause, prepositional phrase, three varieties of complex sentences, appositive

Punctuation: capital, end marks, colon, semi-colon, comma, indent, quotes, apostrophe.

Pick one or two Brainies that will be the day's focus. Make the illustrated gestures as you teach. For example, if you picked the capital letter Brainy, you would make the capital letter gesture (raising one hand above the other) as you started each sentence in a short lesson. Ask kids to use the selected Brainies when they are teaching each other. Reading, writing, any classroom activity involving language, can provide opportunities for Brainy practice.

In traditional education, when we use words like "capital letter," "adjective" or "preposition" the concepts remain abstract, difficult to grasp. *What, on earth, is a preposition?* However, when we represent these terms as cartoon pictures of gestures, the concepts are transformed into an entertaining sign language. Three of the brain's most powerful learning regions are activated by Brainies: the visual cortex (seeing), motor cortex (movement) and limbic system (emotions). A consistent, upbeat use of Brainies will nourish your students' critical thinking, speaking and writing talents. As I said earlier, the more brain areas involved in learning, the more learning takes place.

Now, how to turn Brainies into a high energy game? You'll note in the download, that each Brainy has a point value. A capital letter is worth one point; an appositive is worth five points. The more complex the Brainy, the higher its value. To play the Brainy Game, one of my favorites, give the class a topic and one minute to prepare. Then, for four minutes, select random students. Each pupil speaks a sentence on the topic, using the highest value Brainies possible. To keep score, you simply place a checkmark beside each gesture on your laminated Brainy sheet. At the end of four minutes, total the points. Your kids are learning to think quickly, listen carefully, construct well organized sentences, punctuate correctly and employ complex, logical connectors.

Connecting Brainies to the Super Improver Team

Brainies provide many opportunities for rewards on the Super Improvers wall. Tom, for three weeks, never used a Brainy gesture and look! He's starting every sentence he speaks to Troy with the capital letter Brainy! Super Improver Star for Tom! Harriet uses Brainies all the time when she's teaching her neighbor, but now the dear girl is plunging forward with If-then, a brand new Brainy in her writing. Super Improver Star for Harriet!

For the highest motivation, tape the game and send it to our Brainy League Director, ChrisRekstad@WholeBrainTeaching.com. He'll give you an official score and post it on our YouTube channel. Let your kids compete with other Brainy classes across the nation!

For video examples of *The Brainy Game*, see the Resources on page 38.

Now, let's examine one of our first, and most popular, classroom motivators, the Scoreboard.

3. THE SCOREBOARD

The Super Improvers Team addresses individual growth; the Scoreboard focuses on your class as a whole. If you turn the Scoreboard into a living, video game complete with levels, you'll amp up student engagement to an unbelievable degree. We've designed 10 levels that can be used from kindergarten through high school. Students climb to a higher level by scoring 10 Class Wins (defined below). It's Class Wins, as you'll see, that make the Scoreboard irresistibly challenging and a powerful yearlong motivator.

The positive side of the Scoreboard is labeled two grades higher than the current grade; the negative side is labeled two grades lower. Thus, students are always pointed toward advanced academic achievement.

Make tallies on either side of the Scoreboard as appropriate. Are your students slow in getting out their math homework? Mark a Frowny and call for a Mighty Groan. Is the whole back row intently engaged in independent reading? Mark a Smiley and ask for a Mighty Oh Yeah. Did Maria, bless her heart, patiently help Matthew when he was confused about his map work? That's a Smiley for the whole class, courtesy of Maria. Always keep the score between the positive and negative sides within three points. Reward for class, group or individual behavior. However, never mark a Frowny, for one student's inappropriate actions. The class may object at the penalty, and then the Scoreboard has caused, not solved, problems.

The tally system works to the degree that it is used. Shoot for about

10 marks total, positive and negative, for every hour of instruction. At the beginning of the year, 15 marks per hour would not be unusual.

The sample Scoreboards below are for third grade. For middle school or high school, change the Smiley/Frowny labels to one of those suggested on page 73.

Level 1: *Rookies:* A Class Win is scored when, at the end of the day, there are more positive than negative marks. A tie score or more negative than positive marks, of course, is not a Class Win. *At all levels, the reward for 10 Class Wins is moving up a level.* Thus, it could take 15-20 days, depending on your ability to keep your kids motivated at Level 1, before they earn the joyful privilege of climbing to Level 2.

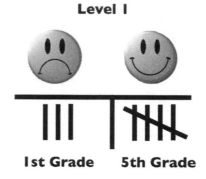

Level 2: *Girls vs. Boys:* From here forward, a Class Win is only scored when both sides end the day with more positive than negative marks. For example, the girls, in a come from behind victory, beat the boys by 1 point and the boys end with more negative than positive marks. Yea, girls! But no Class Win. The next day, the girls beat the boys by three points, both sides have more positive than negative marks. Yea, girls! And, everyone scores a Class Win. One more time: a Class Win is scored when both sides have more positive than negative marks; 10 Class Wins and your kids climb to the next Scoreboard level.

Pitting Girls against Boys dramatically increases the magnetic power of the Scoreboard. *Stay at this, and every, level, as long as possible.* Remember it's a long year!

Level 2

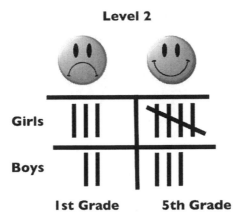

Level 3: *Firsties:* From here forward, all Scoreboards are Girls vs. Boys. For Level 3, the new twist is that whenever it's time to line up, winners go first. Strange but true; I've even found teachers at our conferences are motivated by the privilege of lining up first. *Come on! We've got to beat table three to the snack bar!!*

Level 3

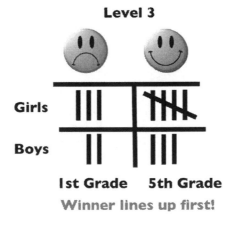

Level 4: *Blue Dubs:* Same as Level 3, but Blue Marks (Dubs) count double, double on the Smiley or the Frowny Side! You'll discover the power of this level when the class falls silent... and all you've done is pick up a blue marker.

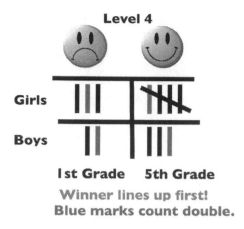

Level 4

Girls

Boys

1st Grade   5th Grade

Winner lines up first!
Blue marks count double.

Level 5: *Leaders Rule:* Same as previous, but each day (or week), the teacher picks two to four leaders for each team. As often as possible, the instructor gives these selected students leadership training in WBT techniques. Leaders' names are added to the Scoreboard. These special kids are occasionally given 30 Second Time Outs, when they can coach their team on winning strategies. Special attention is paid to the leaders' behavior for positive marks.

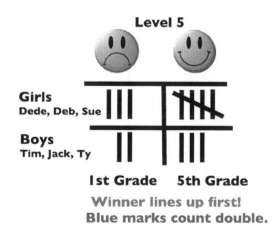

Level 5

Girls
Dede, Deb, Sue

Boys
Tim, Jack, Ty

1st Grade   5th Grade

Winner lines up first!
Blue marks count double.

Level 6: *One Bonus Brainy:* Same as previous, but the teacher selects a Bonus Brainy each day. Girl and Boy teams score points when they consistently and cleverly use the Brainy when teaching each other or responding to the teacher. Note that the Brainies have various point values. The Capital Letter Brainy is worth 1 point. The Triple Whammy Brainy (see page 39) is worth 15 points. Thus, if a high scoring Brainy is selected by the instructor, using this Brainy will increase a team's chances of scoring Blue Dubs (blue marks that count for two points).

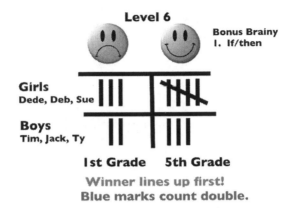

Levels 7-9: Same as previous, but the number of Bonus Brainies doubles at every level. Thus, there are two Bonus Brainies at Level 7, four Bonus Brainies at Level 8, Eight Bonus Brainies at Level 9. Below is a Level 7 Scoreboard.

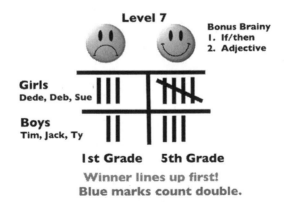

Level 10: *Nightmare Snake Eyes:* at the start of the day, one of the leaders from the previous day's winning game, rolls the dice. The roll determines the number of that day's Bonus Brainies. Thus, a roll of

seven means there will be seven Bonus Brainies. The big twist at Level 10 is that, after learning the dice roll, *each team selects their own Brainies.* Selection strategy is crucial to winning. Mixing low scoring Brainies, that are easy to use, with high scoring Brainies that will impress the teacher, will take each team a few minutes to decide. If 2 (Snake eyes) is rolled, the teacher chooses the Brainies (selecting only the most difficult to use correctly!).

Brain Fact:

The great enemy of instruction is habituation. Repeat the same stimulus enough times and the mind becomes immune to the stimulus.

Eat chocolate cake every day of the week, and by Friday spinach looks tasty.

Because of habituation, the mind's resistance to repeated, identical stimulus, the classroom rewards that produced cheering in September are greeted with yawns in November.

The goal of video game designers is to overcome habituation. This is why video games, and Whole Brain Teaching's Scoreboard, are designed with levels; new stimulus is always one level up.

Scoreboard Summary

- Beginning at Level 2, all competitions are Boys vs. Girls.
- Beginning at Level 3, the reward becomes lining up first (and continues for the rest of the year).
- Beginning at Level 4, all Blue Marks count double.
- Beginning at Level 5, leaders are selected daily by the teacher and their names are added on their team's side of the Scoreboard. Leaders are encouraged to call occasional Time Outs

(three maximum per day) to coach their team on high scoring strategies. Training of leaders by the instructor continues to the end of the year.

- Beginning at Level 6, the game focuses on students using Brainies selected by the teacher. Using higher scoring Brainies frequently when teaching their neighbors is more likely to score points for a team.

- At Level 10, students select their own Brainies, the number based on a dice roll. Kids are encouraged to choose a clever combination of easy to use, low scoring Brainies and more ambitious, high scoring Brainies. If the roll is Snake Eyes, however, the teacher picks the Brainies (always picking the most challenging Brainies, of course!)

If you want alternatives to Boys vs. Girls, pit the right side of the class against the left side, or the first half of the alphabet (based on kids' last names) against the last half of the alphabet, or pick the teams yourself, mixing and matching stronger with weaker students, or simply go back to the pattern in Level 1. If you'd like to give your leaders more power, which is probably a good idea, let them select half the Brainies (and you choose the other half) from Level 6 onward. If you're familiar with the Guff Counter or the Independents, you can make these separate boxes, add-ons, at any point in the game (for a description of these two powerful motivators, see our manual, *Whole Brain Teaching for Challenging Kids* on Amazon.com).

Connecting the Scoreboard to Super Improvers

Because of the motivational power of the Super Improver Team, we strongly suggest tying the Scoreboard and as many other activities as possible to moving up the Super Improver ladder. Thus, when the class advances from Level 1 to Level 2 on the Scoreboard, everyone gets two Super Improver stars. When they advance from Scoreboard Level 2 to Scoreboard Level 3, everyone wins three Super Improver Stars, and so forth. Thus, your students' gaze is always focused on the brightest orbs in Teaching Heaven, Super Improver Stars.

Now, let's stop for a moment and consider the interrelationship between our first three games: Super Improvers, Brainies and the Scoreboard.

Our top three games solve a fundamental problem of classroom motivators... they never wear out. If you've taught for a year or two, you've discovered that prizes that make students cheer in week one, produce yawns by Halloween. Ah, remember how much they loved Friday popcorn parties? After the 5th party you're desperate; what's next, handing out Disneyland tickets?

The beauty of Super Improvers is that every child, your slowest to your fastest, wins. The prize is sweetly intrinsic; the reward for moving up is that you moved up (and everyone can see!!)

Forget popcorn! I used to be a Rookie but now I'm a Starter! Next week I'll be an All Star!

Teachers, again and again, tell us that a mysterious learning energy is unleashed, when students are rewarded for breaking personal records. The fastest kids are desperate because if they don't keep growing, they'll be swamped by the slowest kids. The slowest kids are ecstatic because they are finally in a race they can win.

So, use Super Improvers as your yearlong, individual reward system. Kids are continuously rewarded for being better than they thought they could be.

Brainies solve a different problem. We need a way, a simple, entertaining way, to develop students' intellectual skills no matter whether they are exploring place value, analyzing a plot, or constructing a narrative essay. Brainy gestures provide kids a visual system that encompasses critical thinking, grammar, and punctuation. Brainies can be employed whenever we want our students to think, speak and write carefully... which is all day!

The Scoreboard is a set of ongoing mysteries. Who will win today? Who will line up first at recess? How do we earn a positive Blue Dub and avoid, oh no!, a Negative Blue Dub? What will the next level hold? The teacher waits, happily waits, for the first child to ask, "What do we get if we win?" Your answer is ready, "My dear friend! You receive the same reward as in a video game. Win enough times and you climb to the next level!!!"

4. LEADERS RULE

As you've seen from Level 5 of the Scoreboard onward, we place considerable value in student leaders, the most under-utilized resource in education. We've got bright, charismatic kids and leadership training too often involves handing out papers and cleaning the whiteboard. Developing student leaders becomes imperative when you're teaching teens, or any rambunctious age group.

The first thing you need to discover is the identity of your leaders.

Ask your students to write down the names of three kids in class who they would invite to their birthday party. At home, look over the names. The students with the most invites are your potential leaders.

On another day, hold a discussion about the characteristics of Positive and Negative Leaders (parents, teachers, bosses, coaches, peers). You'll be delighted to see that your students' values are the same as yours. No one thinks a Good Leader is a liar or believes a Bad Leader is considerate.

On another day, reveal the list of Good Leader characteristics that your students mentioned. Then say, "An important part of this class is leadership training. Write down the names of a few kids who you believe would be Good Leaders. I'm looking for students who would have the characteristics on your list."

Take as long as necessary to ponder the nominees. Show the list to colleagues and solicit their input. Then, make the final selection.

Go into the class, and with a flourish, place the list of leaders on your desk. Say, "if we work hard today, maybe we'll have time at the end of class to announce the leaders and have a little celebration." Let the suspense build. Before the period ends, explain a crucial point. *The class did not elect leaders, the leaders were nominated.* You made, and will continue to make, the final decisions. The leaders serve for a period of two weeks. Then, a re-nomination occurs. Explain that you may add, keep or delete leaders. Announce the chosen few and encourage cheering. Talk to your leaders briefly and set up a time for their first training.

Meet with your elite group as often as possible. Review immediate and long term teaching goals. Give your student leaders advance versions of lessons. Solicit their assistance in involving resistant learners in classroom activities. Over several weeks, model the behavior you want in the Class-Yes, Hands and Eyes, Mirror Words, Teach-Okay, the Five Rules, etc. Often in class, use leaders to model excellent WBT behavior. *Leadership training works, if there is plenty for leaders to learn...* their substantial task, motivating for leaders in its size and complexity, is to become Whole Brain Teachers.

When your class is ready for an increase in motivation, place the leaders' names on the Scoreboard. Occasionally add tally marks to the leaders' names indicating their positive activity. Goodness! Those leaders are really helping their team win!

As the game unfolds, it will become obvious to your students which leaders are doing a good job... and which aren't pulling their weight. Every two weeks, hold a re-nomination. Switch leaders, enlarge the group, change seating or responsibilities as you think necessary. Who are you? The merry Leader of Leaders!

5. PRACTICE CARDS

An odd, but powerful entertainment (for teachers), Practice Cards is a game your kids won't want to win. After your students have mastered the 5 Rules + A Diamond, you initiate call outs. A child breaks Rule 2; you say, "Rule 2"; your students exclaim, "Raise your hand for permission to speak." Continue this, consistently, for several weeks and you'll see incidents of rule breaking decline. However, odds are that you will still have kids who need additional rehearsals.

Practice Cards Online
Webcast 565
http://goo.gl/ZRTfSs

Make a display with library card pockets like the following, with each student's number or name.

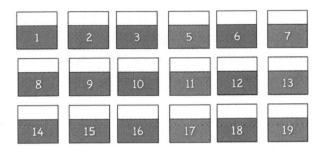

When a rule is broken, pop a white card with the rule number in the student's slot on the Practice Cards display.

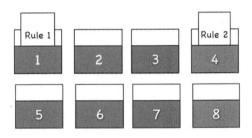

In the past, we've suggested that at recess, the selected students spend two minutes silently rehearsing the rule gesture. Two minutes feels like forever while you're watching other kids play.

Recently, we've had success with a counter-intuitive strategy, giving rule breakers more, not fewer, choices. In traditional education, disruptive kids are given stern directions... go to the office... you've got detention... go sit next to the wall... no choices for you!

We believe that what challenging kids need most is practice in making smart decisions. If this makes sense to you, say something like the following to your class, "As you know, Rule 4, Make smart choices, is one of important rules. If I place a Practice Card in your card pocket,

I'm not angry at you. You simply need more practice with a rule. As you've seen in our class, we learn everything by practicing! However, each of you knows whether you need a longer or shorter rule practice. You know you best. So, at recess, I'll give you the choice between 30, 60, or 90 seconds of practicing the rule gesture. You choose and explain to me why you think you made a smart choice."

Astonishingly enough, in early trials of this method, kids choose 60 seconds of practice more often than 30! Our Beloved Rascals seem to buy into this version of Practice Cards, because they are the ones shaping the rehearsal that is best for them.

Whether you choose the older or newer recess strategy, never give more than two practice cards, per day, to any child. Research indicates that segmented practice, short rehearsals over several days, produces more learning than massed practice, longer rehearsals over fewer days.

Send a note home explaining which rule has been broken. If the note does not come back signed, the student practices for another day. If it is clear to you that there is no hope of getting a signed note returned, assign the child an On Campus Guardian. The note is given to this person who counsels, and consoles!, the child as appropriate. Using On Campus Guardians ensures that all our students have at least one responsible adult in their life.

After a month or so, add a purple rule card, denoting successful behavior. When you see a child following a rule that had previously caused difficulty, pop a purple card in her pocket. Send a note home praising the child for her improvement.

On the first day of class, begin the Scoreboard. No later than week three, start the Super Improvers Team. Wait as long as possible, even until after Christmas, before starting Practice Cards... remember, it's a long year!

Quickstart Practice Cards: Having suggested you wait until after Christmas to start Practice Cards, let me add a footnote. If you have a tough class and several weeks of classroom rule rehearsal shows little behavior improvement, assign your most resistant kids one minute rule practice at recess. Don't put up the card pocket chart, send a note home,

or use the On Campus Guardian. Save those strategies for later. Just initiate brief rule practice and try some of the following techniques.

6. LONG TALK, SHORT TALK OR PLAN TOGETHER

Often, maybe a few times a week with a group of Beloved Rascals, we take a student aside after class for a chat. Following our strategy that challenging kids need smart choice practice, the student is given three options: Long Talk, Short Talk, or Plan Together.

Explain to your class, "If you choose Long Talk, I'll do all the talking, repeating myself over and over, explaining the problem with your behavior. I'll talk until you look like you're weary of hearing me talk and then I'll talk some more. On the other hand, if you choose Short Talk, I'll still do all the talking but I'll speak briefly, clearly explaining the problem with your behavior. *However, I prefer Plan Together.* It's more mature, treats you with respect, values your input. No one knows what you need better than you. If you choose Plan Together, we talk together and make a plan about how to make your classroom experience more rewarding. At some point, it may be a good idea to put our plan in writing so that it will be easier for us to check to see if it is working."

This technique works well with teens, especially if you role play the three choices in class. Pick a lively, agreeable student. Present the three options and demonstrate each. After several days when the pattern is understood, switch roles. The lively kid is the teacher; you become the Beloved Rascal.

A good rule, suggested by Lori White, a Suffolk, Virginia administrator, for any one-on-one, behavior correction session with a student is, "Use I language." In other words, you don't want to hear your student talk about anyone but herself or himself.

7. WRONG WAY-RIGHT WAY PRACTICE

One of the most common questions at conferences begins, "What do you do if..." The blank is filled in variously, (kids don't follow Rule 1, students always shove in line, everyone scribbles instead of neatly coloring). Our most successful strategy for teaching kids the right way to do something, is to first, rehearse the wrong way... and then the right way.

To kinders you might say, "Okay, take your first sheet of paper and show me how preschoolers, who don't know how to work carefully, would make a scribbly mess .... Oh, that's wonderfully messy work! Now show me very careful, second grade work."

To any grade you might say, "I want you to be as slow as snails getting out your math book and opening to page 97... Ah, what wonderful snails you are! Now, show me lightening fast, without tearing pages, how to get out your geography folders and open to the world map."

A wonderful feature of rehearsing the Wrong Way is that it is a no-fail activity for your most resistant kids. When you tell them to break Rule 2, "Raise your hand for permission to speak," and just start chattering... what challenging activity is left to them... polite hand raising???

Wrong Way-Right Way practice only takes seconds, but vividly clarifies what isn't, and what is, appropriate classroom activity, without scolding.

The previous two strategies, Long Talk, Short Talk, Plan Together and Wrong Way/ Right Way Practice, are powerful, simple strategies that only take a minute or so to implement. They are short fixes for what may be long term problems. The next two strategies, Classroom Engagement Average and Challenging Kid Average are yearlong techniques that address virtually every classroom management problem from advancing your most gifted students to reforming your Beloved Rascals. Think of these as solitaire games; you play them on your own and won't need to twist any student arms.

8. CLASSROOM ENGAGEMENT AVERAGE (CEA)

Classes change and improve, but usually at the pace of a glacier. You need a way to convince yourself that you're getting somewhere!

The beauty of the Classroom Engagement Average is that you play it in solitude. A teaching game with no instruction involved!!

Go through your roll and, privately, score each pupil as follows:

- **Alphas:** These model students look at the one who is teaching, follow directions quickly, raise their hand for permission to speak, stay on task, give you their best effort. Give each Alpha a 4.
- **Go-Alongs:** These kids frequently follow the lead of the Alphas. They usually look at the one who is teaching, follow directions quickly, often raise their hand for permission to speak and, normally, stay on task and give you their best effort. Give each Go-Along a 3.
- **Fence Sitters:** One day a Fence Sitter is with you every step of the way, the next day he is flinging erasers across the room. Fence Sitters inconsistently look at the one who is teaching, follow directions quickly, raise their hand for permission to speak, stay on task or give you their best effort. Score each Fence Sitter a 2.
- **Challenging Kids:** A genuinely challenging student rarely, if ever, looks at the one who is teaching, follows directions quickly or anything else you wish them to do. Give each Challenging Kid a 1.

(As a quick index of where to place a student on this scale, think about the Diamond Rule. Alphas almost always look in the right direction; challenging kids often look elsewhere.)

Mark new pupils as Fence Sitters, until you get to know them better.

Add up all the scores and divide by the number of students. This will give you your Classroom Engagement Average (CEA). For example, if the total points of all your 30 kids is 90, then your CEA is 3.0 (90/30). *Perform this calculation weekly.* The engagement of your students improves… but often at a rate that is microscopic, to slow to notice daily.

Your goal is to raise your CEA by .1 every month; over a 10 month school year, you will have moved every student up a level. If you diligently follow the two steps below, student leaders and star cards, your CEA will rise higher and faster.

Student leaders: Train your 4s to be classroom leaders. As described previously, meet with them daily if possible; teach them WBT techniques you use in class. Train your Alphas to be rule leaders and demonstrators of new Whole Brain strategies. Give these special kids advance lessons in Brainies. As your 4s become adept at skills you use in class, you've created a new category. Give yourself a 5 for each Student Leader. Work on moving 4s to 5s because it's sensible to address the easiest to solve problems first. Your 4s want to be 5s! Yea!

As you transform 4s to 5s, seat them with 1s. Think of 5s as assistant teachers. You've got challenging kids... you need lots of help.

Every two weeks, ask the class to nominate classmates who would be good student leaders. Use these suggestions and your own intuition to increase the size of your leadership group.

Your eventual goal is to train two 5s for every 1. Then, bracket your challenging kid, if any are left, with two of your most popular student leaders. If Wild Jack still refuses to participate, then he will, nonetheless, be bombarded by the energy of two, merry neighbors.

Star Cards: Assess your 3s, 2s and 1s, and pick a handful, probably not more than five, who are the closest to moving up a point. We'll call these kids Climbers; your intuition tells you they're ready to climb higher, Challenging to Fence Sitters, Fence Sitters to Go Alongs.

Give each Climber a Star Card labeled with one behavior you want her or him to polish. Say, "If I see consistent growth in this area, I'll give you a Super Improver Star!" Tell Climbers to record a tally mark on their card whenever they think they are doing a good job hitting their target behavior. Explain, "Show me your cards at the end of the day. When I'm convinced you've formed a new, positive habit, the Super Improver Star is yours!" You'll find that having kids self-tally simplifies your oversight tasks. Your students do the record keeping; you merely take a few seconds at day's end to inspect the results.

Do not specify the number of tally marks required for a Super Improver Star. If you make that mistake, your kids will quickly record the tallies and stop trying to improve!

Do not, do not, do not award a Super Improver Star if a child has not significantly improved their target behavior. Your goal is not to be nice, but to provide objective assessment of what is praiseworthy in your class.

Occasionally, drop by a Climber's desk with a star hole punch (a hole punch that cuts out a star shape.) As you cut a star into the delighted Climber's card say, "Good job. Star punches count as double tally marks."

When other students see the Star Cards you're giving the Climbers, they will clamor for their own. This clamor is the celestial music of Teaching Heaven. Say, "Work hard on the Diamond Rule (or another goal of your choosing) and maybe you'll get a Star Card of your own." Oh, yes! Kids begging to self tally their own behavior improvements!

So, to significantly raise your Classroom Engagement Average follow these steps.

- Calculate CEA weekly, noting your 4s, 3s, 2s, 1s.
- Train your 4s to be 5s and seat these student leaders with 1s.
- Select a small group of 3s, 2s, and 1s for Star Cards and have them tally their successful implementation of a behavior that will advance them on the Super Improvers wall.

Every week or so, change the Climbers group. After five days, many Climbers will have tallied an amazing 50+ incidents of their target behavior. Well worth a Super Improver Star. There is a good chance that after only a month, many of your kids will have advanced to a higher level!!

If you have an extremely tough group with a high percentage of challenging kids, add the Challenging Kid Average to your Classroom Engagement Average.

9. CHALLENGING KID AVERAGE (CKA) *LEAD*

You have the toughest of the tough classes, or a knot of kids that, frankly, drive you bonkers.

Here's your motto:

Control what you can control.

You can't always control the pace at which your kids, especially if they are challenging, acquire learning skills... but you can always control the teaching strategies you use to help them acquire learning skills.

Let's think more about the difference between a learning skill and a teaching strategy.

A learning skill is an ability your students use to acquire knowledge. Reading and writing are two, obvious, learning skills. A teaching strategy is a tactic you use to help your students acquire learning skills. Many of the games you have explored thus far in this book are teaching strategies. The Super Improvers Team and the Scoreboard are teaching strategies that help your student acquire learning skills. Here are a few more examples: a phonics game is a teaching strategy to improve the learning skill of word decoding; skip counting is a teaching strategy to improve multiplication skills; giving choices with Practice Cards is a teaching strategy to improve classroom behavior.

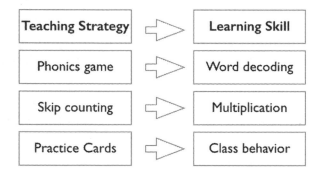

Now, huge point. Really huge.

You can enormously reduce your anxiety about instructing challenging kids if you understand that *teaching strategies are under your control.* You may not be able to instantly foster a learning skill in a resistant learner, but you can, always, choose which teaching strategy to use. *Your primary worry is not whether or not a child is acquiring learning skills but how well you've employed a teaching strategy.*

I'll make that point again.

Confronted by a challenging class or driven up the wall by a few tough kids, you must stop losing sleep. Don't worry about resistant learners themselves; concern yourself about your implementation of strategies to help resistant learners.

Control what you can control.

You always control your teaching strategies; you can't immediately control the speed with which your students gain learning skills.

After 15 years of training teachers, I'm convinced that America's education problem is not our students' poor learning skills but teachers' shallow reserve and haphazard application of teaching strategies. Educator's have too few teaching tricks up their sleeves and apply them inconsistently. Teachers are obsessed with challenging behavior instead of perfecting their pedagogy.

In general, you can assess the quality of the educators at your school by listening to their conversations. The unhappiest and least successful teachers talk about their rowdy kids. The happiest and most successful teachers talk about instructional strategies. Miserable instructors see classes full of students who lack learning skills. Productive instructors see classes full of students who will respond to new instructional strategies.

Here are two case histories to make the distinction clearer between a teaching strategy and a learning skill.

Early in the year, second grade instructor Katie H. is alarmed to note that Tom, one of her students, has never, in his life, written a word without assistance. Writing is the learning skill Tom lacks. Katie tries various teaching strategies, haphazardly. She talks to Tom's parents, but doesn't follow up. Katie sits with Tom and encourages him, but she has lots of other needy students. She tells Dianne, her teaching assistant about Tom's problem, but Dianne is not a talented student motivator. Katie frets about Tom's writing problem, but she should be fretting about her inconsistency in applying a teaching strategy to help her second grader. Katie needs to understand that serious learning problems are solved slowly. She needs a plan to guide her plans!

Harry B., a middle school history teacher, has a tough class. Lots of kids interrupt him, never turn in homework, could care less about Harry's passion for the Civil War. Harry, wisely, sees that his students' lack of learning skills requires a disciplined set of teaching strategies.

Harry worries about what he can control, the careful application of tactics to help his kids learn. So, Harry decides that he will train student leaders. That's his teaching strategy... and a wise one. Many of his kids, maybe all of them, want to be leaders. Harry's problem is not to coerce students into acquiring learning skills, but to devise and *continuously assess* his own ability to implement the teaching strategy of training student leaders. Harry knows this will take time. Every week he assesses his own student leadership training strategy, rating himself from 4 (highest) to 1 (lowest). As he revises his tactics, his self-rating scores climb. *Harry's primary focus is not his kids, but his own ability to implement and revise his instructional tactics.* After six weeks, some of his kids become leaders and Harry, along the way, discovers new techniques for leadership building.

When your back's against the wall, don't panic. Pick a teaching strategy, give it time, keep assessing your implementation effectiveness.

To calculate your Challenging Kids Average, look at your class roster and make a list of students who are 1s and low 2s. Pick one or two teaching strategies from the list below that you think will help reform your Beloved Rascals.

1. Rules are entertainingly rehearsed five times a day.
2. Wrong Way/Right Way rehearsal of one rule accompanies every rule practice.
3. You consistently use rule call outs.
4. A minimum of 10 tally marks are recorded on the Scoreboard for every hour of instruction.
5. At least one student per day receives a Super Improver Star.
6. 4s receive training at least three times per week in becoming 5s. 5s are seated with 1s.
7. Star Cards are employed with a small group of Climbers.
8. Students who consistently break a classroom rule, practice the rule at recess.
9. Practice Cards are implemented for the class as a whole (with a special focus on challenging kids).

10. You regularly employ Long talk/Short talk/Plan together.

11. You use the Bulls Eye Game (page 130) daily with a few challenging kids.

For example, you decide to focus on three resistant learners: La-Donna, Jim and Carlos. As a teaching strategy, you select Long Talk/Short Talk/Plan Together to employ with each of the three. A second strategy, Wrong Way/Right Way practice, will be used with the class as a whole, paying special attention to its effect on your three tough, but nonetheless, Beloved Rascals.

As mentioned, controlling what you can control, your assessment, will be on your ability to implement the strategy, not on its immediate success.

	Long/Short/Plan	Right/Wrong/Practice
LaDonna	4-3-2-1	4-3-2-1
Jim	4-3-2-1	4-3-2-1
Carlos	4-3-2-1	4-3-2-1
AVERAGE		

You rate (4 highest-1 lowest) your implementation skill daily.

After talking to LaDonna about her three choices (Long Talk, Short Talk, Plan Together) you unhappily realize that you used a harsh tone and picked an occasion when you didn't have the time needed to chat with her. Though the encounter did seem to make a positive impression on the girl, your implementation rated a 2.

You faithfully used Wrong Way-Right Way practice three days in a row, several times per day. It was difficult to judge, over such a short period, the effect of the practice on your three challenging kids. Nonetheless, you believe you did a good job of implementation. You give yourself a 4.

And so forth, for several weeks, even months. Tough kids can, miraculously, make a quick turn around... but ordinarily their behavior improvements take considerable time. (In fact, if a challenging kid quickly improves, she wasn't challenging at all... a pseudo-challenger! Oh, for a class of Imitation Toughies!)

Oddly, the limitations of the CKA are its strengths. Given your time constraints, you can only select a few challenging kids and you can only try a few strategies. Good! Less truly is more. The fewer resistant learners you select and the fewer strategies you employ, the more likely you are to achieve high scores for implementation. Never give up on a teaching strategy until you have successfully implemented it for at least two weeks. Some teachers report it takes 8 to 12 weeks of consistent WBT implementation before improvements are noted.

Here's the great news. No matter how challenging your students, if you use the CKA faithfully, you are guaranteed to become a better educator. What is more wonderful than that? Month after month, as you diligently self assess, you increase your ability to successfully implement teaching strategies... and that skill is precisely what you need when dealing with challenging kids (and the rest of your class).

Final note: with all your students, your most effective strategy for increasing your Classroom Engagement Average and your Challenging Kid Average is the Super Improvers wall. No matter whether you are using CEA or CKA, give your 1s exceedingly simple, individualized targets for improvement. Don't say to Wild Jack, "Be considerate of the rights of others." Such a direction is nebulous; the wisest philosophers would disagree about what your request involved. Instead say, "Jack, it would be an improvement if you kept your hands folded, like the other kids, when we line up for first recess. I'm only looking for this at first recess, but I'd love to see it in the lunch line!"

Now, before we go on to our last of our top 10 games, let's review the first nine games and include my best guesses for timeline guidelines.

1. **Super Improvers:** powerfully nourish individual social and academic growth by rewarding for improvement and not ability. (K-12: Day one).
2. **The Scoreboard:** motivate your class as a whole by turning classroom management into a yearlong, multi-level game. Remember: motivate individuals with Super Improvers, the class with the Scoreboard. (K-12: Day one).

3. **Brainies:** Incorporate writing and thinking skills into any language activity. (K-12: Day one).

4. **Leaders Rule:** Develop student leaders with the goal of training them to be Whole Brain Teachers of their classmates. (K-1: Week 6-8: 2nd-12: Week 4-6)

5. **Practice Cards:** Implement rule gesture rehearsal for Beloved Rascals. (K-6: try to hold out until after Christmas!, use Quickstart Practice earlier)

6. **Long Talk, Short Talk. Plan Together:** A strategy for one-on-one counseling with resistant learners. (K-12: probably no sooner than week 4. This game only works if you've previously established a talking relationship with the selected student.)

7. **Wrong Way/Right Way Practice:** Teach students the correct way to follow a procedure by rehearsing the incorrect way. (K-12: Should only be employed after at least 4 weeks of daily rule practice. K-3: rule practice can be every few hours for weeks, before the Wrong Way/Right Way game is played.

8. **Classroom Engagement Average (CEA):** Evaluate and improve every student's engagement in learning. (K-12: Weekly after the first month).

9. **Challenging Kid Average (CKA):** Assess your implementation of teaching strategies, not success, with your Beloved Rascals,. (K-12: As needed, week 2 onward).

As stated at the beginning of the chapter, most of the entertainments in our top 10 involve classroom management. Now, how about an irresistible learning game?!

10. MIND SOCCER

There are thousands of classroom games, but few create more exuberance than a well designed round of Mind Soccer.

Draw a horizontal line along the bottom of your whiteboard and mark it off in five equally spaced vertical lines, hash marks. This is your Mind Soccer field. Place an eraser below the middle hash mark. The eraser, of course, is the soccer ball.

Prepare a list of 50 or so short answer questions, reviewing important class material. Examples: The top number in a fraction is _____ . The longest river in Africa is _____ . Robin Hood lived in _____ .

Divide your class into two teams... girls against boys works wonderfully. Select a captain from each side (don't let the kids pick captains, it takes too long).

The captains stand in the front of the room, a desk between them (same set up as TV's *Family Feud*). You ask a question. The captains slap their hands down. The one who is first and answers correctly wins the kickoff.

> **Mind Soccer Online**
>
> Webcast 507
> http://goo.gl/s1ggfm
>
> WBT YouTube
> http://goo.gl/QuOkxK

The captains go back to their teams. You fire a question at the winning team. They shout back the right answer. You move the eraser slightly toward the opposing team's goal. *The ball is moving down the field!* What a good kick! Attackers cheer... defenders groan... loudly!

Another question for the attacking team... another right answer... the eraser ball moves down the field. Cheering! Groaning!

You fire another question... right answer... but too slow! The other team gets possession! You fire questions at them. The ball, ah yes!, moves the other way! Ha! Ha! Former cheerers are groaning now... and former groaners are cheering! Back and forth! Back and forth! Wait... what was that? Someone complained?

The teams learn the One Dreaded Rule of Mind Soccer. **Keep the Ref happy!** The complaining team is penalized. However you want. The ball is moved... or a free kick is awarded... or a point is deducted. None dare complain. Keep the Ref happy!

Eventually, a goal is scored... pandemonium breaks out. The game continues.

Mind Soccer can be a reward for anything... everyone turned in their homework! Hurray! The class advanced to the next Scoreboard level! Hurray! Our test average is over 75%! Hurray! We win three minutes of Mind Soccer!!!

Use a timer. The shorter the game, the more your kids will beg you to play again.

Contemplate this. Your students will work hard on any class goal for the mere privilege of playing a game that reviews course material!

Want to take student involvement over the moon? After an especially intense game of Mind Soccer, award everyone a star on the Super Improvers wall.

Your students don't dig soccer? Call it *Mind Football.*

Now, think back over our top 10 games, but don't be overwhelmed. You can go a long, profitable distance with just the first three: Super Improvers, The Scoreboard and Brainies. Add others as needed. One thing about Whole Brain Teaching... you've got a big back pocket.

Now, let's add a few more classroom management games before we go on to writing, reading, math, Common Core and challenging kids.

The games you've learned about thus far that you think will be most useful to your kids are: ___Mind Soccer___
___Long, Short talk 8 & 9___

_____

_____

The easiest game to implement will be: _____

because ___Mind Soccer — something___
___new and different___

_____

_____

_____

At this point in your exploration of this text, the best advice you can give yourself is: don't be afraid to try these strategies and don't give up until you have time to assess what you are doing.

CHAPTER 4

Classroom Management Games

If it's not fun, it's not Whole Brain Teaching.

— BIFFY BLUEBIRD

In this chapter, you'll learn entertaining variations on the Big Seven: Class-Yes, Mirror Words, the Scoreboard (more tweaks!), the Five Classroom Rules and the Diamond, Teach-Okay, Hands and Eyes, Switch and other strategies that will turn your class into a learning fun factory.

CLASS-YES!

Our Attention Getter, Class-Yes, is probably our most popular strategy. You'll use it all day long and so you'll need ways to keep the call out engaging. Last thing any teacher needs is a lifeless Attention Getter. Spend some time at home, practicing different tones of voice, pacing and inflection on the following.

> **Class-Yes Online**
> Webcast 514:
> http://goo.gl/855u6B
> WBT YouTube:
> http://goo.gl/BR5LEj
> http://goo.gl/GkvimB

11. Class-Yes Variations

Here are 20 variations on Class-Yes.

1. *Cowboy:* Class Yee-haw! (Your class responds, "Yes Yee-haw!" The same echoing pattern is used for the rest of the variations.)

2. *Backward Cowboy:* Haw-yee Class!
3. *Mouse:* Class Squeaky!
4. *Hipster:* Yo Class!
5. *Ninja:* Class Saaaaa-eeee!
6. *Gangster:* Class Badda Boom!
7. *Urban:* Waz-up-wichoo Class!
8. *Surfer:* Gnarly Class!
9. *Corny Surfer:* Cowabunga Class!
10. *Sweetie:* Classy-Wassy-Dinkums!
11. *Marine:* Ooorah Class!
12. *Sergeant:* Class! Atten-hut!
13. *Strict Teacher:* Backs Straight Class!
14. *60's Motown:* Banana Fanna Class!
15. *Cheerleader:* Class Shacka Lacka!
16. *Zombie:* Yummy Nummy Class!
17. *Lovey Dovey:* Class Smoochy!
18. *Lewis Carrol:* Mimsey Class!
19. *Hippie:* Righteous Class!
20. *Beatles:* We all live in a yellow submarine, Class! (Your class responds, probably laughing, "We all live in a yellow submarine, yes!")

The key to using these variations is not to employ them too frequently, about 3-5 times per day. Whenever you need a burst of merry attention, surprise your kids with a new, Class-Yes personality.

12. Class-Yes Echo Leaders

Pick several kids, as many as a third of your class. These are your echo leaders.

> **SCRIPT: Echo Leaders**
> **Teacher:** Classity-Class-A-Bing-Bong
> **Students:** Yessity-Yes-A-Bing-Bong
> **Teacher:** (puts one hand behind each ear, as if listening for an echo)
> **Echo Leaders:** Yessity-Yes-A-Bing-Bong

You often have to say "Class" more than once, so involve some kids as your echo... which will make them hyper-attentive to your initial Class-Yes call out.

13. Name-Yes

The idea of *Name-Yes* is that you teach your students that whenever you call their name, they respond, quickly with "Yes!" and look at you.

"Juan!"

"Yes!" (hands folded, looking at you)

"Tina!"

"Yes!" (hands folded, looking at you)

Juan's a good kid, on task, but you called his name to set up Tina who was off task. *Name-Yes* is a strategy for pulling an off-task student quickly back into your lesson.

Spend time modeling the lightening speed that you are looking for in your students' response. (Some of my colleagues change "Follow directions quickly" to "Follow directions immediately.")

It's simple to turn Name-Yes into an entertaining and remarkably powerful game. Set aside a 10 minute period in the morning, make a tally mark, or ask a student leader to make one for you on a piece of paper at their desk, each time you use *Name-Yes*. Write this score on the board. In the afternoon, tell your kids that their goal is to have fewer tally marks than in the morning. Name-Yes is like golf, the lower the score the better. In other words, the goal is to have as few students off- task as possible.

To make the game even more entertaining, ask several other teachers, at any grade level, to record tally marks for the 10 minute morning period. Then, at noon, find out what the scores are in the other classes. After lunch, all the classes involved will try for the new lowest score.

At the beginning of the year, keep victory celebrations short... maybe a 10 second victory dance by kids and teacher. As the year unfolds, try a few minutes of *Mind Soccer* (see previous chapter) to mark victories.

MIRRORS

As you recall, Mirror Words is one of our primary instructional techniques. You say, "Mirror Words" and pick up your hands. Your kids respond, "Mirror Words" and imitate your gestures. You can act out the parts of a story, visually illustrate core concepts, demonstrate a science experiment with imaginary tools.

Mirror Words is so powerful that you'll use it often. Keep the technique fresh by occasionally using one or more of the following.

> **Mirrors Online**
>
> Webcast 533
> http://goo.gl/bcz2MU
>
> WBT YouTube
> http://goo.gl/BDUXJE
> http://goo.gl/QJBGOz

14. Mirror Words Variations

Here are 10 variations on Mirror Words:

1. Giant Mirror Words! (Your kids respond, "Giant Mirror Words" and imitate your gestures. The same pattern is used in the rest of the variations.)
2. Tiny Mirror Words!
3. Rabbit Fast Mirror Words!
4. Turtle Slow Mirror Words!
5. Mirror The Words Right Now!
6. Mirror Wacky Words!
7. Right Hand Mirror Words!
8. Left Hand Mirror Words!
9. Calm and Quiet Mirror Words
10. Arms Way Out Wide Mirror Words!

Play any of these 10 characters while using Mirror Words:

1. *Cowboy:* Saddle Up Yer Words!
2. *Lovey Dovey:* Mirror Words, My Little Sweeties!
3. *Mouse:* Squeak My Words!
4. *Monster:* WORDS! GRRRR!
5. *Newswoman:* Breaking News! Mirror These Urgent Words!
6. *Southern:* Y'all Mirror My Words!

7. *Robot:* Words Mirror, Words Mirror!
8. *Pirate:* Arrg Maties! Unfurl Yer Mirrors!
9. *Indecisive:* Mirror Words? Words Mirror?
10. *Computer:* Download Mirror Words App!

Judiciously use these variations of Mirror Words, just enough to keep kids engaged. Employ the above, as necessary, to wake up a drowsy morning class or energize instruction on a long afternoon.

15. Great Big Point

Post a large sign in the front of the room, "Great Big Point" with a down-pointing arrow. When you stand under the sign, you're ready to present an important message. Then say, "All rise!" Your kids stand up; you use Mirror Words, make Great Big Gestures, and announce your Great Big Point. Think of the Great Big Point sign as a cheap, powerful spotlight.

16. Silent Mirror

In WBT, we use three types of mirrors. In Mirror Words, students say our words and imitate our gestures. In Magic Mirror, (game 17) students say our words but create their own gestures. In Silent Mirror, students mimic our gestures but don't say our words. One more time!

Mirror Words: You speak and gesture; your kids repeat your words and gestures.

Magic Mirror: You speak but don't gesture; your kids repeat your words and create their own gestures.

Silent Mirror: You speak and gesture; your kids say nothing but repeat your gestures.

The special power of Silent Mirror is that kids improve their listening skills. They focus intensely on what you're saying, preparing to teach their neighbor your lesson.

17. Magic Mirror

In Magic Mirror, you speak slowly with your hands behind your back. Kids repeat your words but create their own gestures. Thus, if you're telling a story about a mountain climbing expedition, kids create their own mountains in the air, imaginatively inventing gestures to illustrate key moments in the tale. If you're discussing Aboriginal life in Australia, students invent movements to bring your description to life. An excellent variation of Magic Mirror, is to have one of your liveliest students stand beside you. As you talk, she invents her own gestures, which the class mimics.

Got a Beloved Rascal who loves attention? Have a talk with her and say, "I'd love to see the stuff you dream up if you were the Magic Mirror Leader. If you could just follow the Diamond Rule a bit better, I'll make it happen. Whenever you want during recess, remind me how well you're doing."

18. Wigglies Up

Kids get antsy. You exclaim, "Wigglies up!" Any student, who likes to move around, can stand. Then, use Mirror Words to teach a lesson. When you're finished, the standing Wigglies use big gestures to teach their neighbors.

As you and your class become more proficient in using Mirrors, you can switch from one to another, mid-lesson. Think of this as Whole Brain Teaching's equivalent of a square dance, with you playing the role of the caller. Instead of dosey-do and swing your partner, you start with Mirror Words, whirl into Silent Mirror and finish up with a grand round of Magic Mirror.

Next, let's think more about the Scoreboard. You'll use this remarkable game many times a day, all year. The levels, described earlier, will change the contest enough to keep it continuously engaging. However, it's always a good idea to have more tricks in your back pocket. In WBT, our back pocket has a back pocket.

THE SCOREBOARD

19. Optional Scoreboards

As a supplement to the Scoreboards described in Chapter 2, you can get surprising mileage out of simply changing the names of the positive and negative sides (with corresponding sounds.) Pirate (Arg!) vs Crew (Yo, ho, ho!), Turkey (gobble, gobble!) vs. Farmer (Yum! Yum!), Empress of the Universe (students silently bow in your direction) vs. Earthlings (Yipee!), etc.

For secondary students, put the name of your school on the positive side of the Scoreboard and a rival school on the negative side. When the rival school scores, kids exclaim "Ugh!" When your school scores, everyone gives the Marine cheer, "Oooo-rah!"

> **Scoreboard Online**
>
> Webcast 522
> http://goo.gl/OsCYZu
>
> WBT YouTube
> http://goo.gl/1sNs84
> http://goo.gl/wP5pV8

19. Scoreboard Rewards

We suggest you don't use *any* Scoreboard rewards, except lining up first... for as long as possible. When absolutely necessary, hopefully no sooner than January, you can supply additional motivators. If you're playing Girls vs. Boys, and there are more positive than negative marks on both sides at the end of the day, reward with one minute extra recess, or one page less homework, or any other small bonus. This works wonderfully if you also indicate that more negative marks than positive will result in one minute less recess or one page more homework.

Remember this general principle for Scoreboard bonuses: the smaller the reward, and the harder to win, the more valuable the prize.

20. Scoreboard Bonus

To add still more variety to your Scoreboard, indicate a bonus behavior that you'll be looking for.

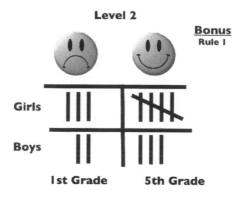

In this case, you'll be adding positive points for following directions quickly. Rule 2 also works well as a bonus, because it's one of the most difficult principles for kids to follow and one of the easiest to monitor. Also, as you've seen, Brainies provide a large supply of bonus possibilities.

21. Mobile Scoreboard

WBT had a Scoreboard app, but discontinued it when we discovered how often Apple upgraded their operating system. Many teachers create a portable Scoreboard by placing a card inside a clear plastic nametag holder. They carry the Mobile Scoreboard with them suspended from a lanyard. It's then a simple matter to record positive and negative tallies with a marker. Not only does this work well in the classroom, saving you from travelling to the main Scoreboard, but also the Mobile Scoreboard accompanies you as your class moves from one campus location to another.

22. Mystery Road

Draw a long, windy road on the whiteboard. Mark various stops with question marks and exclamation marks. Place a large Star at the end of the road. In place of positive and negative marks, use a dotted line to record your students' journey along Mystery Road. Positive behavior... ah! Draw the dotted line on the road, moving toward the Star. Negative behavior... no! Draw the dotted line off the road, oh no! The dots are heading back to the finish, far, far from the Star. In advance, decide what happens when the dotted line arrives at a question mark or exclamation mark (a quick test, a review of classroom rules, a new activity, announcement of a future event, preview of a video, etc.). Arriving at the Star... which may not happen on the first day's journey, can signal a new game.

What new game?

You have 122 to choose from.

23. Commandantes Arriba!

When your kids need variety, replace the Scoreboard with a leadership game, and teach your English speakers a bit of Spanish. On the whiteboard, under the heading Commandantes Arriba!, list your classroom leaders. Whenever they engage in positive behavior praise them, and get everyone to exclaim *Ole!* Occasionally, tally a positive mark (no negatives in Commandantes Arriba!). When your marvelous commandantes reach 10 points (near the end of the day), stop and play a game of *Mind Soccer*... or any other WBT game.

TEACH-OKAY

Let's stop our journey and describe how Class-Yes, Mirror Words and Teach-Okay can be linked together to form magnetically engaging lessons.

Teach-Okay Online

Webcast 516
http://goo.gl/rJFxfP

WBT YouTube
http://goo.gl/pZf59G
http://goo.gl/FLxnjf

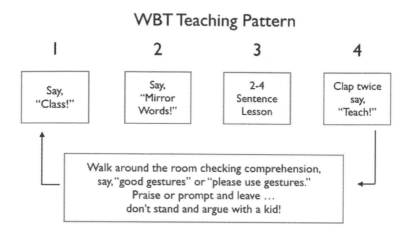

At 1, above, use any variation of your Attention Getter. For simplicity, I've selected "Class!" Your students respond "Yes!"

At 2, you say "Mirror Words" and pick up your hands. Your students respond, "Mirror Words" and pick up their hands.

At 3, you teach a short lesson, using gestures. Your students repeat your words and mimic your gestures.

At 4, clap twice and say, "Teach!" Your students clap twice and say, "Okay!" and teach your lesson to a neighbor.

Then walk around the room, listening to students paraphrase your brief lesson. If they understand, go on to your next point; if not, re-teach.

As you can see, Class-Yes, Mirror Words and Teach-Okay form a smooth continuity. With the variations you've learned of the first two techniques, and what you'll soon discover about Teach-Okay, this instructional sequence can be endlessly various and irresistibly engaging.

24. 1,000 Teach-Okay Variations

Teach-Okay is our version of think-pair-share, an opportunity for students to review their instructor's lesson with a neighbor. For increased fun, we like to begin with a sound effect, like clapping one or more times. We've also seen teachers use finger snapping, desk knocking and head patting. You make the sound effect, then say, "Teach!" Kids repeat the sound effect, say "Okay!" and teach a neighbor your lesson.

I hope you're convinced that the more fun kids have learning, the more they will learn. Hand clapping or finger snapping is like sprinkling your lesson with Silly Powder. Butterflies love nectar; kids love Silly Powder.

Believe it or not, here are 1,000 variations (10x10x10) of the Teach-Okay sequence! Let me know when you've tried them all; we'll write the next WBT book together.

Preface	Teach request	Voice
Clap 1-5 times	Teach!	Mousy
Desk knock 1-5 times	Teach-rooski!	Marine
Pat your head	Yabba-dabba-teach!	Cowboy
Any dance move	Hi ya! Teach!	Serious
Wave hands overhead	High energy Teach!	Wacky
Wiggle your fingers	Wiggly! Woggly! Teach!	Frightened
Foot stomp	Yo, teach!	Susie Sunshine
Karate move	Teach yazoo!	Baby Lala
Robot arm wave	Smarties teach!	Super Hero
Any two of the above	Teach Boom!	Sports Announcer

You seize your students' attention with a lively Class-Yes. Next you present a brief lesson, just a few sentences. Then, you're ready for Teach-Okay. Pick an item from column 1, Preface; combine it with an item from column 2, Teach request, and employ a voice from column three. Your kids repeat your preface, insert an "Okay" for your teach request and mimic your voice.

25. The Learning Train

Think about the number of times you say something like the following, "John keep your hands to yourself... Martine stop playing with your tassels... Adele please look at me... Davey don't bother Andy." These are typical, ongoing corrections while teaching most classes.

The problem is that you are stopping a lesson for 30 kids, to gain one child's attention. One of our newer mottos in WBT is, *Don't stop the train.* Class begins, the Learning Train starts rolling. And keeps on rolling, chug-chug-chug teaching, for the whole period. Don't stop the train to coax one kid back on board.

Unless it is a safety issue, do not halt a lesson to address an off task student. Finish your lesson, move into Teach-Okay, and then, while your kids are using gestures to paraphrase your points to a partner, go over to the to the student who is off task and provide correction. *Guide individual kids back on the train, while the whole class is still rolling!*

26. Sockless Hand Puppets

You may have a student, Wild Jack, who works better alone.

Wild Jack isn't keen on talking to his neighbor during Teach-Okay. Have him pick up his hands and use Sockless Hand Puppets to teach himself your lessons. The Speaking Sockless Hand Puppet jabbers to the Listening Sockless Hand Puppet. Insist that they take turns, treating each other politely. Follow the Golden Hand Rule. Treat your right hand like your left hand wants to be treated. The Listening Sockless Hand Puppet nods when it understands the lesson but balls up into a fist when it is lost.

If Wild Jack isn't comfortable teaching a neighbor, ask him to teach himself, with his puppets, during Teach-Okay. Or, weirdly effective, suggest your Beloved Rascal teach his shoe.

27. Shoe Buddy

Kids who are lone wolves often love teaching their shoe. Sticking out one foot, Wild Jack uses energetic gestures during Teach-Okay, directed at his attentive foot. Shoe Buddy waggles whenever a difficult point is clarified. Wild Jack, happily, keeps making his Shoe Buddy smarter.

28. 1,010 Teach-Okay Variations

Okay, you're a wonderfully fast learner and you've mastered the 1,000 Teach-Okay variations in game 24. Here are ten more.

1. Two foot stomps, "Go!"- Students stomp twice and exclaim, "Okay!"
2. A disco move, "Rock!" - Students mimic your dance move and say, "Okay!" In all the following, your kids imitate you and then respond, "Okay!"
3. Whirl an invisible lariat over your head, "Lasso!"
4. Monkey scratch under your arms, "Ooga-ooga!"
5. Assume a Super Hero pose, "Vic-to-reee!"
6. Bongo beat a desktop, "Dig it!"
7. Pretend like your tearing a huge sheet of paper, "Let 'er rip!"
8. Elvis imitation, "Viva Las Vegas!"
9. Air guitar imitation, (guitar sound effects!)
10. Turn an invisible car key, "Vroooom!"

29. Teach-Okay Inventions

In the classic Teach-Okay, you clap twice, say "Teach!" Your kids clap twice and say "Okay!" Then, as I've said, they turn to teach your lesson to a neighbor. However, you may want them to start a new activity, reading or writing, for example. Clap twice and say "Read!" or "Write!" No matter your instruction, their response is always "Okay!" If you're working on Brainies, then you would cue them with "Brainies" or, perhaps, "Adjective" if you've selected that Brainy for focus. Or, you might say, "Props!" meaning, your kids should use a prop, usually a pencil, to represent some aspect of a lesson, a long river, a Mars bound rocket, a timeline.

30. The Swoop

Difficult to describe, but wonderful to behold, the Swoop is so advanced, I may be the only one to ever use it. Here's what I say to my college classes, "I'm going to clap twice and say 'Swoop!' You clap twice, and turn away from your neighbor, faking like you're going to teach someone else. Then you say, 'Ooooo-kay!' and suddenly turn back to your partner and start teaching like crazy with big gestures." Correctly executed, the Swoop provides big laughs. Everyone turns one direction and then swoops back in the other and teaches like crazy.

HANDS AND EYES

As you remember from Chapter 2, we use Hands and Eyes as a preface to our big announcements. We exclaim, "Hands and Eyes!" and rapidly fold our hands. Our kids respond, "Hands and Eyes!" and rapidly fold their hands. Just for the pure pleasure of it, we stare at each other for a moment... happy teacher, magnetized class. Ah! Then proclaim the big announcement. This technique is so effective, I often have big announcements every five minutes.

> **Hands and Eyes Online**
>
> Webcast 519
> http://goo.gl/UGRIXF
>
> WBT YouTube
> http://goo.gl/sm7GXI

"Hands and Eyes!"

Kids reply, "Hands and Eyes!"

"Never forget that the bottom number in a fraction shows how many parts in a whole!!!"

Or,

"Mrs. Johnson claims her class is quieter, more mature than our class. We're going on Ghost Recon down the hall and *they won't even know we're there!*"

Or,

"Every paragraph in your essay must start with a topic sentence!"
And so forth.

31. Hands and Eyes Escalation

For an enormously important point, say "Hands, hands, hands and eyes!" For the biggest possible announcement, say, "Hands, hands, hands and eyes... Aiiii" In both cases, your kids repeat what you said and rapidly fold their hands.

32. Hands and Eyes Mime

If you use an extremely expressive facial expression and large gestures, you can silently mouth the words "Hands and Eyes." Your kids should silently mirror you and fold their hands, ready for your big (spoken) point.

33. Hand and Eye

When you have a short announcement, and are feeling wacky, say, "Hand and Eye!" Cover one eye with one hand; your kids do likewise. Make your short announcement.

Want wackier?

Try something like, "Right pinky and left ear lobe!" (Touch your left ear lobe with your right pinky... make your announcement.)

Next, let's look at two games that guarantee that all students are involved in peer instruction. No players on the sidelines!

SWITCH

As with everything else in the WBT Fun Factory, we want kids to enjoy taking turns teaching each other. Of course, there is a difference between having fun learning and having so much fun learning that no learning takes place. Remember, we to use a pinch of Silly Powder, not a handful! If kids get too carried away with Switch or any other game, then use the Scoreboard to model the Wrong Way (too goofy, like kids in a lower grade) and the Right Way (just the right amount of fun, like students in a higher grade.)

Switch Online

Webcast 522
http://goo.gl/WspxWM

WBT YouTube
http://goo.gl/XAeHOT

34. Three Switches

When students are teaching each other, one is the Speaker and the other is the Listener. There are several ways partners can change roles. The instructor can call out "Switch!" and the kids reply, "Uh oh, Switch!" and pull down one arm, as if pulling down on a giant switch. Or, when the Speaker finishes her lesson, she can give the Listener a High Five Switch (clapping hands in mid-air). Or, for variety, students can delicately touch the tips of their pinkies and whisper, "switch."

35. The Hygienic Flop Switch

At a recent Missouri conference, one teacher objected to students slapping hands because of "the germ issue." Okay. Wind-up like you're going to give your neighbor a big High Five, but swish your hands past each other, dramatically, hygeinically, missing.

THE FIVE RULES + A DIAMOND

Here are, again, our five classroom rules and the principle that is so important we call it the Diamond Rule.

Rule 1: Follow directions quickly.
Rule 2: Raise your hand for permission to speak.
Rule 3: Raise your hand for permission to leave your seat.
Rule 4: Make smart choices.
Rule 5: Keep your dear teacher happy!
♦ **The Diamond Rule:** Keep your eyes on the target.

Now, let's look at ways to gamify (yes, it's a word) our rules.

36. Rule Leaders

One of the simplest, most widely used, techniques for helping students learn our rules is to employ Rule Leaders. (A great task for the 5s described in the previous chapter.) Pick an outgoing kid, ask her stand up and callout each rule number. The class responds with the gesture and rule itself.

> **Classroom Rules Online**
>
> Webcast 559, 560
> http://goo.gl/xI4c9L
> http://goo.gl/CFy4OS

The girl exclaims, "Rule 1." Her classmates respond, "Follow directions quickly!" Encourage, and model, the use of wacky voices: frog, robot, monster, Squeaky the Mouse or Quacky the Duck. Your most challenging kids, hungry for the spotlight, will often eagerly reform their behavior to be rewarded with the role of Rule Leader. What child can resist being Quacky the Duck?

When approached by a challenging student, begging you to let her be a Rule Leader, say kindly, "Rule leaders are good rule followers. Tell me which rule you're going to work on before first recess."

37. Stopwatch 1

Time your students' transitions and put the records on the board. How fast can we line up without trampling each other? How quickly can we all get out our yellow geography folders *and* our colored pencils? Can we beat our backpacks-in-the-cubbies record?

37. Stopwatch 2

Try using a stopwatch to see how long your class can go without breaking a rule three times. (This works especially well for Rule 2, "Raise your hand for permission to speak"). We give students three tries because we don't want to come down heavily on one student. When the rule is broken the first time, say, "that's one!" Write the time on the board. Encourage with, "Let's see if we can go longer before someone forgets and breaks the rule again." After the third occasion when the rule is broken, write the total time on the board.

Say, "Okay. That's good for a start. Next time we play let's see if we can do better." Try this for a week or so and then propose a new challenge... "Let's see how long we can go without breaking the rule twice!"

Michelle Holt, one of our WBT Texas interns, discovered that, on first playing this game, her kids only made it to 22 seconds... before they'd broken Rule 2 three times! That's rowdy Texan energy!

38. Stopwatch 3 With Wondrous Feats

Pick a challenging time goal, like going 30 minutes without breaking rule 2. *Promise your kids that if they can achieve this amazing goal, you'll perform a wondrous feat.*

When they meet your goal, wait until a few minutes before the end of the day. Gather everyone around and perform any card trick that you find online. A lovely and simple trick is to have a child pick a card, show it to everyone else but not you. Cut the cards and have the kid place the chosen card on top of the bottom stack. Steal a glance at the card that is on the bottom of the *top* stack.

One more time.

You hold the deck in your left hand. You pull off a stack of cards in your right hand. The child puts her card face down on the left hand stack. As you put the right hand stack on top of her face down card, sneak a glance at the card on the bottom of the right hand stack. When you put the cards back together, the card you glanced at, the Marker, will be on top of the card the child picked.

Then do your mind reading routine. "I'm getting an image of a black card. No, it's a red card. It's a card between 3 and 7. No wait, it's a queen... I think." Convince the kids that you are wacky. It's amazing how easy that is.

Slowly deal the cards out, turning each one face up. Go past the Marker by several and then dramatically say, "The next card I turn over will be the chosen card." Of course the kids will think they've fooled you. Then go to the cards already laid out and turn over the card before the Marker, the card the student chose.

An even better trick, and one well worth mastering, is Catch-the-quarters-falling-off-the-elbow. This one sounds impossible but it can be mastered in 10-20 minutes practice at home. Bend your right arm (if you're right handed) and place the back of your right hand above your right shoulder. Your right elbow should be about parallel to the ground, level enough to hold a quarter. Place the quarter on your right elbow and then, in a smooth motion, *no hesitating,* swing your cupped right hand down and, with practice, you'll catch the falling quarter. Do not try to deliberately catch the quarter, don't bounce your elbow, just swing your cupped hand down. The quarter will fall straight; you intercept it. This is a wonderful trick, but amazingly enough, when you can catch one quarter... two is just as easy. A quarter and a dime, which sounds more difficult because the coins are different size, is just as simple.

Now listen!

Catching five, ten, fifteen stacked coins is equally easy. I'm a klutz but I've caught 28 stacked coins, so dream of that. The cool thing is that you can keep expanding this trick... "Okay, today if you can go 45 minutes without breaking Rule 2, I'll try to catch two quarters, two nickels *and two pennies!*" Kids will try this trick at home and beg you to let them demonstrate. Fine. "Okay, today, if everyone can go 55 minutes without breaking Rule 2, we'll let Wild Jack and Lucky Lulu demonstrate their elbow quarter skills."

39. The Brainy Minute

We want our kids to think critically, about everything, even our rules. The core of WBT's critical thinking curriculum is the Brainy "Because."

"Because" links statements to supporting evidence.

I love Whole Brain Teaching (statement) *because* it is fun (supporting evidence).

"James and the Giant Peach" (statement) is a great book *because* you can never guess what will happen next. (supporting evidence).

We must revise our essays carefully (statement) *because* we are always striving to improve our writing skills (supporting evidence).

Frequently during the day, give kids a Brainy Minute to orally fill in the following as many times as possible in 60 seconds:

_____ because _____ .

For example, "Rule 1 is a good rule because _____." "Rule 4 is important to remember on the playground because _____." A good rule would be _____ because _____."

The Brainy minute and "Because" can also, obviously, be used for other critical thinking tasks.

"Booker T. Washington was a great man because _____."

"College will be exciting because _____."

The Brainy Minute can be employed to give students a choice between pro and con positions.

"*Of Mice and Men* is/is not a great novel because _____."

"Computers do/do not make life easier because _____."

"Everyone should/should not go to college because _____."

Perhaps best of all, use of The Brainy Minute develops students' ability to speak Triple Whammies (see game 91). Students might spend the entire minute, or more, revising sentences like these:

"The South was doomed to lose the Civil War because _____ , _____ , and _____ ."

"Three ways to improve our environment are _____ , _____ , and _____ ."

"The best life goals are _____ , _____ , and _____ ."

40. Choose Your Rule

Say, "Hold up your fingers, 1-5 and show me which rule you think we can do the best job following in the next hour." Select the rule that wins the most votes and write the rule number as a bonus (see pg. 41) next to your Scoreboard. Marking positive and negative tallies, pay close attention to how well the rule is being followed. When students choose a rule, you can be fairly sure they'll do a good job following it.

Brain Fact:

The prefrontal cortex, the brain's reasoning center, does not fully develop until the early 20s. This is why children often make irrational (emotional) choices. Your students are not "bad," they are under-developed pre-frontally. The more practice you give kids in making smart choices, Rule 4, the more you nourish the growth of their brain's reasoning center.

---

41. Rule Roll 'Em

Say, "I'm watching to see who does the best job of _____ [pick whatever behavior you want]. A student who does a really good job, will get to roll the Rule Dice!" Teach for awhile and then pick the Rule Roller.

We have five rules plus the Diamond Rule. Your selected student rolls one die. (Weird, but kids will do almost anything for the privilege of rolling dice.) The number that comes up, 1-6, determines the rule you'll use as the Scoreboard bonus rule for whatever time period you select.

42. The Big-Blink-A-Roo

Once your kids have learned and reviewed the Five Classroom Rules and the Diamond, it's time for The Big-Blink-A-Roo. Whenever during a lesson you tightly close both eyes, your students must say the rules and make the gestures as quickly as possible... certainly before you open your eyes. If they perform this wondrous stunt, give them two positive marks on the Scoreboard (the only time this happens!). To make the gag even more entertaining, open one eye. This will make your kids speed even more madly forward.

43. The Ka-Ching Leader Box

As stated in game 1, our primary goal in WBT is to reward students for improvement rather than ability. The Super Improvers Team rewards students for an ongoing pattern of improvement in social or academic skills; the Ka-Ching Leader Box provides a supplementary reward system for smaller improvements. Big improvements? Super Improvers Team. Small improvements... a glimmer of an improvement? Ka-Ching Leader Box.

Here's what the Leader Box, looks like:

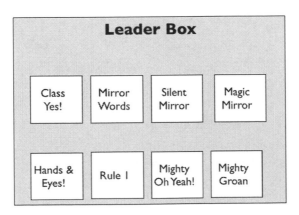

On the outside of the box, glue library card pocket holders labeled with whatever WBT call-outs you frequently use.

Put each student's name on five cards. Thus, if you have 30 students, you will have 150 cards. Arrange the cards alphabetically, or any other way, so that you can quickly select a kid's card. When you note improvement in any academic or social skill, drop the pupil's card in the Leader Box. If you see ongoing improvement during the day, a kid's card can be dropped into the box again and again. When a student's card is dropped into the box, the class says "Ka-ching" followed by the pupil's name. Thus, Juan gets a "Ka-ching Juan!," Mary gets a "Ka-ching Mary!"

No kid on Earth can resist the Ka-Ching.

Whenever you wish, dramatically draw a card, the lucky card, from the Leader Box. Place the card in one of the card pocket holders. After several names are drawn, the outside of the box will look like this:

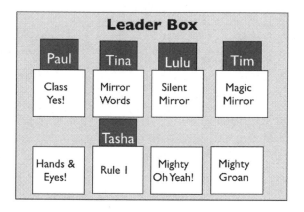

The selected students get the delightful privilege of being a call-out leader during the day. When you nod at Tina, she exclaims "Mirror Words!" and the class responds, "Mirror Words!" When you point at Tasha, she exclaims, "Rule 1" and the class responds, "Follow directions quickly!" The reward for improvement is that the student becomes a classroom leader for a day.

Occasionally, model how rapidly the class should respond to the leader callouts. Empty the box at the end of the week.

On Friday, say to a challenging child, "If I could see you improve (name an easy to improve behavior) on Monday, then your name *will be the first one in the box.* But do help me. I may forget, so remind me Monday morning." *This will give your Beloved Rascal something to think about all weekend!*

The following game doesn't fit neatly under the category of the Five Rules, but it addresses a central instructional problem, focusing on a few kids and neglecting others.

44. Spread the Love!

Some of your students, especially your Beloved Rascals, receive more than their fair share your attention (worry, sleepless nights, extra doses of chocolate). Other students, usually the quietest, rarely receive adequate attention. Stop stressing about your Rascals. Every child deserves the same amount of your concern.

Make a 3 x 5 card for each student. Sort the deck so that top cards are the pupils who have received the least attention; kids on the bottom have received the most. As you teach during the day, smile at, pat on the back, say a few encouraging words, to the students on the top of the stack. Gradually sort them to the bottom, bringing new pupils into view. Every child is starved for attention; feed the ones first who you have rarely invited to your table. Top carders are your daily focus. Spread the love!

Now that we have some indications about classroom management and daily instruction, let's look at a crucial academic activity, writing. I taught composition for 40 years and never found a sound method until two years after I retired! My four decades of struggles are your gain.

CHAPTER 5

Writing Games

I write to discover what I know.

— ST. AUGUSTINE

Every Whole Brain classroom is a writing lab. As a general strategy, begin every lesson on any subject with a question that the lesson will answer. What is a verb? What is a musical scale? How do you solve quadratic equations? How did the Agricultural Revolution change human society? Then, at the end of the lesson, the writing task is straightforward. Students write a detailed answer to the lesson's question.

To turn this all purpose writing assignment into a game, play *Etheria*.

45. Etheria

On the other side of the Sun, where we can't see it, spins the Mystery Planet of Etheria. As Earth moves, Etheria moves... the sun always blocking our view. Etheria looks very much like Earth, similar continents, rivers, mountains. Etherian society has had a history very much like ours, evolving from primitive hunter-gatherers to video game lovers.

Unfortunately for the Etherians, they have no schools!

All the great advances in Etherian civilization have been made by Lookies. A Lookie passes into a trance to see what is happening on Earth... and reveals this valuable information to the rest of Etherian society.

Have a good time (tongue in cheek) explaining all this to your students. Etherians love the Earth... they want to know, are desperate to know because they have no schools, everything about Earth Ways.

Say, "We just had a lesson on verbs. The question was, 'What is a verb.' Now, write a letter to the Etherians answering that question. Teach them everything you've learned about verbs, give them lots of original examples, use your Brainies! Teach those poor, desperate Etherians! Tonight I'll mail your letters via UPE, United Parcel Etheria. *Maybe I'll hear from them tomorrow with more questions for you about what we're learning!!!*"

If you wish the letters to be clearly structured, put an outline on the board describing what each paragraph contains (see *Triple Whammy* below).

Of course, when you note improvement in students' Etherian letters, you reward them with a Super Improver star.

If writing to Etheria is an all purpose, composition assignment, then the Triple Whammy sentence is an all purpose, topic sentence.

46. The Triple Whammy

A key component of Whole Brain Teaching's essay writing method is the Triple Whammy topic sentence. The Triple Whammy is so versatile that it can be learned by the end of kindergarten and usefully employed through high school. I wish I'd found this marvelous composition device before I retired from teaching!

> **Triple Whammy Online**
> Webcast 542
> http://goo.gl/qEAWmK
>
> WBT YouTube
> http://goo.gl/yp7nTc
> http://goo.gl/77Qmge

Here is a sample Triple Whammy topic sentence.

_____ is _____ , _____ , and _____ .

The three blanks can be filled in a variety of ways.

Whole Brain Teaching is *fun, easy to learn,* and *motivates students.*

The Lord of the Rings is *exciting, filled with great characters,* and *wonderful places.*

The Amazon River is *one of the longest rivers in the world, provides irrigation water to tens of thousands of farmers,* and *is becoming polluted.*

The beauty of the Triple Whammy is that each of the three parts can be expanded into a paragraph in the body of an essay. For example, the outline of a composition that would follow the first sentence above would be:

Whole Brain Teaching is *fun, easy to learn,* and *motivates students.*

Paragraph describing the fun involved in Whole Brain Teaching.
Paragraph describing how easy Whole Brain Teaching is to learn.
Paragraph describing how Whole Brain Teaching motivates students.

Using the word "because" transforms the Triple Whammy into the topic sentence of an argumentative essay.

_____ because _____ , _____ , and _____ .

Congress must spend more on education because *the U.S. lags behind other developed countries, many schools are in serious disrepair,* and *children are the future of our nation.*

Ernest Hemingway was a great writer because *his stories were realistic, always described dramatic events,* and *were full of simple, but vivid, language.*

Math problems are difficult because *they often need two or more math operations, require careful reading,* and *are hard to visualize.*

Using color coding helps students understand the structure of a Triple Whammy. Highlight the following with colored markers to show beginning students the structure of a tightly organized paragraph.

_____ because green reason, blue reason, and red reason.
A sentence about the green reason. A sentence about the blue reason. A sentence about the red reason.

A color coded Triple Whammy essay could use a pattern like the following:

_____ because <u>green reason</u>, <u>blue reason</u>, and <u>red reason</u>.

A sentence about the green reason. A sentence about the blue reason. A sentence about the red reason.

A paragraph about the green reason.
A paragraph about the blue reason.
A paragraph about the red reason.
A paragraph about the green, blue and red reasons.

Encouraging students to use pens or pencils that match the color code of the Triple Whammy increases their engagement.

An obvious reason why students write so poorly is that they don't receive enough writing practice. Our solution is to provide hundreds of reps in orally rehearsing good writing skills.

Pair your students, a weaker writer matched with a stronger writer. Give them a minute to take turns orally filling in the following blank as many times as possible.

_____ *because* _____ .

You can assign one or more subjects (California history, the life of Cesar Chavez, playground behavior) or give students free rein to pick their own topics.

When you are satisfied that your kids can fill in one blank after "because," go on to two.

_____ *because* _____ , *and* _____ .

Again, have them take turns filling in the blank as often as possible, setting and breaking one minute team records.

The next step is to move on to the Triple Whammy.

_____ *because* _____ , _____ , *and* _____ .

As students' skill develops with speaking a Triple Whammy sentence, put the paragraph and essay patterns described above on your whiteboard. For every five units of oral practice, include approximately one unit of written practice. You'll see student composition skills improve dramatically.

To make using Triple Whammies orally and in writing, even more productive and entertaining, encourage the use of these Braines: capital letter, and, end mark, because clapper, comma.

Brain Fact:

The brain's most long lasting memories are acquired through the visual and the motor cortex. This is why you remember faces better than names; images of faces are stored in your visual cortex. If you learn to ride a bicycle at seven, and don't ride again until you're ninety... you can still ride a bike. Bike riding memories are stored in the motor cortex. The brain learns best, as in Whole Brain Teaching, by seeing and doing.

---

47. Triple Whammy Ka-Ching

During Teach-Okay, whenever kids speak a Triple Whammy, a three part sentence, they say "Ka-Ching!" hoping to gain the teacher's attention to drop both their names in the Leader Box (see game 87).

Sample Triple Whammy sentence frames:

"The teacher said _____ , _____ , and _____ ."

"The three main ideas we covered were _____ , _____ , and _____ ."

"The most important points we need to remember are _____ , _____ , and _____ ."

48. The Golden Triple Whammy Ka-Ching:

The very best, and most universal, Triple Whammy involves giving three reasons to back up an assertion. "_____ because _____ , _____ , and _____ ." When kids achieve one of these wonders there is a special reward. So that you won't be driven to distraction, students should remember their very best Golden Triple Whammy and tell you at recess. If you think it is an improvement over their previous efforts, they can announce it in class and everyone says, "Ka-Chingy-Ding Ding!" Then, drop two copies of the student's name in the Leader Box!!

49. Stomp that Error!

Teachers spend useless hours proofreading students' papers. It's not educators who need to identify grammatical errors, but students. How well would your own children learn to brush their teeth, if you did it for them?

Stomp that Error! goes a long way in developing student proofreading skills. Find a one page selection of text on the Internet at your students' reading level. Copy and paste two copies of the text into a word processing document. In one copy, introduce errors you want your students to identify. For example, add unneeded capitals and delete capitals that are properly used. Or, remove periods, insert extra commas, delete required commas, misspell easy words... whatever you wish! (However, it's best to start with one proofreading skill and add others as kids' detective abilities advance.) Print the error filled version of the text on one side of a sheet of paper and the correct version on the other. Ask kids to work individually or in pairs correcting errors. After five or ten minutes, tell them to check the marked errors against the correct version. Whenever they have found, and fixed an error, they can stomp their feet twice in joy. Foot stomping is a fine celebration because it's vigorous and not too noisy. We've found foot stomping celebrations are better than tossing chairs into the air or tickling the kangaroo.

50. Sloppy-Neat

To improve handwriting, during in-class writing, ask kids to alternate between writing sloppy and neat sentences. The first sentence is sloppy, the next one neat, the next one sloppy and so forth. Writing sloppy, on purpose, will improve writing neatness!

At the next level, kids write one sloppy sentence and then two neat sentences. For even more careful focus, kids can alternate sloppy/neat capitals, spacing, periods, indenting... or any other writing feature where legibility is imperative. Walk around the room and praise amazingly sloppy handwriting that was followed by wonderfully neat penmanship.

Stop for a moment.

As you page through these suggestions, keep in mind that their educational merit is directly related to their entertainment value. As I've said, the more fun your kids have learning, the more they will learn. For example, with the Sloppy-Neat game just described, try exclaiming, "Oh my friends. Let's do something wacky! All in favor of wacky, say YaZoodly! (Kids exclaim YaZoodly!) Good job. Instead of normal writing, I want you to show me your messiest work! Yes! Sloppy sentences rule! After every messy sentence you create, make the next one so perfect it looks like it was created by the Neat Writing Machine..." etc.

You may be thinking at this point that, properly framed, any class exercise can be entertaining. I agree. Let's start a charter school, Funny Bone Academy.

51. Hawk and Gopher Proofreading

I used this in-class proofreading game for years, but have never had a chance to describe it in print. The strategy was invented because I was going nuts after decades of correcting college essays. This is how I regained my sanity.

First, I put a list on the board of errors I wanted students to mark on their neighbor's papers: capitalization, end marks, misspellings, apostrophe errors, misunderstanding of the assignment, failure to follow the Triple Whammy essay model, etc.

Then, I said, "Give your paper to your neighbor. Beg her or him to mark ALL the errors on the board. Then, when finished, hold up the paper and waggle it slowly in the air. Look around the room. When you see another paper being waggled, like a hawk on a fat gopher, swoop in and trade papers. Keep going until I ask you to stop."

With enough reps, this technique insured that student papers would be filled with corrections. When kids received their own papers back, I'd say, "There are lots of marks on your paper. Put a star beside each error that you agree is an error. However, do not star anything you don't think is an error!" This invariably led to discussion between students and with me, as to what constituted a correctly noted mistake. Excellent teaching opportunity!

As my next step, I'd say, "Now, count up your starred errors and put the number in the upper right corner of your paper. But please pay close attention. If I find an error that has been marked on your paper and you didn't star it... *that will cost you 10% of your grade for each one!*"

Scoring papers at this point was a breeze. The stack had been proofread, possible and actual errors already marked! I'd read through the papers, look at each starred error and see if I agreed. Numerous stars meant lower grades. Excellent papers would have few stars; I'd spend more time reading these carefully, making suggestions for improvement.

Long ago I abandoned split grading, one grade for "content" and the other for "form." It seemed ridiculous to tell a student she had "good content" when her ideas were buried under a coating of grammatical errors. If my students followed the Triple Whammy pattern and had few technical errors, then they received good grades. Good form, following the pattern, was good content.

52. Red/Green Dotty

The problem with writing is that it involves too many skills: capitalization, sentence structure, spelling, grammar, punctuation, effective use of adjectives, adverbs, appositives, quotations... and don't forget apostrophes!

Red/Green Online
Webcast 531
http://goo.gl/1MUHjk

Our kids have a hard time with composition because there are so many concepts that must be remembered. Complex activities from dance to piano playing are typically taught and practiced one skill at a time. Let's do the same with writing.

Give your kids a 10 minute writing task. Say, "Keep writing until time is up." This will keep students from rushing through the assignment. No one is finished until everyone is finished.

Begin by saying, "All I want you to work on today is neat writing. That's it! Just write neatly! I'll walk around with a red and green marker. I'll put a green mark beside your neatest word and a red mark beside your sloppiest word. Give me more like the greens and no more like the reds!"

As the weeks unfold, add the following, in any order, to your Red/Green Dotty list.

- Neat spacing
- Neat end marks (no bowling balls or pinpoints)
- Two sentences in a row cannot begin with the same word
- Grade level sentence length (kindergarten: sentences must be longer than four words; high school: all sentences must be between seven and 15 words)
- Paragraph indenting
- Paragraph length (3-5 sentences)
- Adjective in every detail sentence in the body of the essay (underline)
- And: no sentence begins with, or contains more than one "and."
- Every sentence passes the Midnight Phone Call Test (if you heard the sentence on your phone, at midnight, it would make sense). This is an excellent rule to test for fragments and awkward constructions.

We suggest that students write for 10 minutes every morning and afternoon. The morning writing task can focus on one of the Red/Green Dotties above; afternoon writing can focus on several from the same list. As the range of writing skills among your students becomes clear to you, assign Red/Green goals individually, based on your kids' abilities.

The following three eBooks, *Electronic SuperSpeed Grammar, The Whole Brain Writing Game* and *WBT Writing* are available as downloads at WholeBrainTeaching.com, under "Free eBooks/general."

53. Electronic SuperSpeed Grammar

Electronic SuperSpeed Grammar is a giant order of learning fun. Containing over 600 PowerPoint slides, this mammoth program guides your kids through some of the most challenging material in elementary school... grammar! *Electronic SuperSpeed Grammar,* illustrated with hundreds of cartoon graphics, covers: nouns, verbs, sentences, adjectives, adverbs, prepositions, prepositional phrases, pronouns, articles, conjunctions AND appositives! The program is so lively and colorful, your kids will feel like they're reading a comic book instead of studying parts of speech.

54. The Whole Brain Writing Game

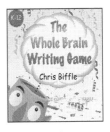

The Whole Brain Writing Game is a WBT's composition system. Using striking visuals, K-12 students learn fundamental writing skills: brainstorming, writing topic sentences, composing paragraphs, constructing narrative, explanatory and argumentative essays, proofreading, use of adjectives, active verbs, descriptive language, prepositional and adverbial phrases, proper use of commas, correct subject verb agreement... you name it! *The Whole Brain Writing Game* is a lively, modular system that can be adapted to any writing program.

55. Whole Brain Writing

Whole Brain Writing, along with *The Writing Game* (described above) contains WBT's complete K-12 writing system. Topics include: simple, complex, compound and topic sentences, tightly focused paragraphs and essays, brainstorming, proofreading, scaffolding from easier to more complex assignments, neatness (!), sentence variety, lessons on nouns, verbs, adjectives, prepositions, adverbs, conjunctions, appositives, motivation to work hard… the whole kit and a giant kaboodle! Whole Brain Writing brings together our most popular, classroom tested strategies, Oral Writing, *Super Speed Grammar, The Genius Ladder,* Triple Whammy Sentences, Red Green Proofreading, and the Super Improvers Team. With new techniques for brainstorming and pre-constructed multi-media assignments, this great program creates a unified, highly engaging program for beginning to advanced writers. Illustrated with a lovable crew of cartoon Mind Giants, our eBook reads like a comic. Don't look through *Whole Brain Writing* unless you have a big hanky. When you're done, you'll be weeping tears of joy!

Stop for a moment. Think back over the writing games in this chapter. List the games below that will help your kids the most.

_____

_____

_____

_____

_____

_____

_____

_____

SEVEN BIG PROBLEMS: Seven Potent Solutions

Okay. We're about halfway through our journey through WBT Playland. I imagine you might be overwhelmed by our learning toys. Good! What's better than having too many ways to have fun teaching?!

I've picked a handful of games you might start with.

Think of our entertainments as solutions to problems. Here are ways to address seven of the most common difficulties I hear about from teachers.

1. **Problem:** your students have a wide range of skills, ranging from Special Ed to gifted.
   Solution: Super Improvers Team.

2. **Problem:** your students speak without raising their hand.
   Solution: Wrong Way/Right Way practice of Rule 2, "Raise your hand for permission to speak."

3. **Problem:** Almost all your kids have weak writing skills.
   Solution: Lots of oral work with Brainies, written letters to Etheria, and Triple Whammy sentence practice.

4. **Problem:** Your students have short attention spans.
   Solution: Amp up lessons with variations on Class-Yes, Mirror Words, and Teach-Okay.

5. **Problem:** Your class, as a whole, is lackadaisical.
   Solution: Get the multi-level Scoreboard rolling!

6. **Problem:** You have too many Beloved Rascals.
   Solution: Assign challenging kids easy to achieve Super Improver goals. Calculate your Classroom Engagement Average and Challenging Kid Average weekly. Begin Long Talk/Short Talk/Plan Together. Wait nervously for the wonders revealed in chapter 9, "Games for Challenging Kids."

7. **Problem:** Kids read slowly with weak comprehension.
   Solution: Turn the page.

CHAPTER 6

Reading Games

*There are perhaps no days of our childhood we lived
so fully as those we spent with a favorite book.*

— MARCEL PROUST

The following reading games, 56-63, are downloads under "Free Ebooks/general" at WholeBrainTeaching.com. Additional reading games, at the end of this chapter, are new to this edition.

56. The Crazy Professor Reading Game

The Crazy Professor Reading Game, one of our first e-books, has also been one of our most popular. Used by thousands of K-12 teachers, the Crazy Professor is designed to deepen students' reading comprehension of fiction and nonfiction. Kids, working in pairs, learn to paraphrase, summarize, ask guiding questions, enliven complex topics with gestures, skim read for key ideas, and connect text to personal experiences. A powerful modification of independent reading, the Crazy Professor works as well with ELL and Special Ed pupils as with gifted students. Once underway, the program runs itself, engaging a whole class or a small reading group. During Open House, a one page handout, included in the eBook, is all you'll need to motivate parents to improve their kids' reading comprehension.

Crazy Professor Online

Webcast 544
http://goo.gl/Mb2Ssq

WBT YouTube
http://goo.gl/Nvz2Fq

57. SuperSpeed Letters and Phonics

SuperSpeed Letters and Phonics is the easy way to teach beginning readers the alphabet, capital and lower case letters, and phonics sounds. Students work in pairs, more advanced kids teaming with less advanced, naming as many letters as possible in one minute. When time's up, teams play again trying to beat their record. Perfectly differentiated, each pair moves at its own pace, but continuously experiences the thrill of mastery as new records are set and broken.

58. SuperSpeed 100

Based on the standard Dolch and Frye lists of the most common words in English, *SuperSpeed 100* significant-ly increases students' fluency. New readers, working in pairs, have a blast as they race through 100 sight words. The words are: the, to, and, he, a, I, you, it, of, in, was, said, his, that, she, for, on, they, but, had, at, him, with, up, see, all, look, is, her, there, some, word, out, as, be, each, have, go, we, am, then, little, down, do, can, could, when, did, what, so, not, were, get, them, like, one, this, my, would, me, will, yes, big, more, went, are, come, if, number, now, long, no, way, came, too, ask, very, than, an, over, yours, its, ride, into, just, blue, red, from, good, any, about, around, want, don't, how, know, part, right, put, sound. Throw away those flashcards... watch in de-light as your kids play *SuperSpeed 100*, feverishly setting and breaking records for reading speed.

> **SuperSpeed 100 Online**
>
> Webcast 511
> http://goo.gl/Ifx4Rf
>
> WBT YouTube
> http://goo.gl/VOctt3

59. Electronic Super Speed 100

Electronic SuperSpeed 100 is the remark-able new version of one of our most popu-lar literacy games, *SuperSpeed 100* (de-scribed above). Your kids will learn sight words, rhymes, consonants, vowels, nouns, verbs, adjectives, beginning and ending consonant blends, simple and complex sentences, even CRITICAL THINKING!!... all in a PowerPoint format. Fully customizable!

60. SuperSpeed 1000

Teach your class 1,000 of the most common sight words. Students will BEG YOU to let them play! *SuperSpeed 1000* is so motivating, middle school teachers have used the game as reward for good behavior. "You kids have finished so much work, with such excellent study habits, that we're going to play *SuperSpeed 1000*." "Yippee!," the students exclaim. This remarkable contest, ample enough for year-long practice, begins with: the, to, and, he, a, I, you, it, of, in. Nine hundred, ninety words later, the game finishes with: stand, track, arrived, located, sir, seat, division, effect, underline, view.

SuperSpeed 1000 Online

Webcast 511
http://goo.gl/lfx4Rf

61. Electronic SuperSpeed 1000

Electronic SuperSpeed 1000 is the PowerPoint supplement to one of Whole Brain Teaching's all time, most popular games, *SuperSpeed 1000* (described above). Increase your students' reading speed of the 1000 most common sight words! As addictive as a video game, *Electronic Super Speed 1000* can be played by kids from early elementary through high school. Use the PowerPoint format to add, subtract and rearrange the slides in the sequence that is best for your students. As a special bonus, we've included *Nightmare Roller Coaster!* What's that??? Download the program, if you dare, and find out.

62. Biffytoons

Biffytoons uses cartoon gestures to teach young learners sight words. This e-book features 48 full color, 8"x10" cartoon posters, 48 8"x10" line drawings for coloring, 48 mini-cartoons to distribute to parents, Biffytoons Bingo for in-class fun, and more! A host of features introduce new readers to the most common words in English. The Biffytoon words are: the, to, and, he, a, I, you, it, of, in, was, said, his, that, she, for, on, they, but, had, at, him, with, up, see, all, look, is, her, there, some, word, out, as, be, each, have, go, we, am, then, little, down, do, can, could, when, did, what. Every Biffytoon word is illustrated by a cartoon gesture. Put the included posters on your wall and your kids will learn to read as easily as if they were looking through a picture book.

63. Electronic Biffytoons

Electronic Biffytoons is a powerful supplement to our Biffytoons eBook. Set up as a PowerPoint for use with a computer projector, you can add, subtract, rearrange the words in the most useful sequence for your new readers. Beginning with "the, to, and..." and covering the 48 most common words in English, every term in *Electronic Biffytoons* is illustrated by a cartoon and gesture. The program is a powerful aid to kindergarteners, English language learners, Special Education students, beginning readers of every age and ability. To avoid injury while viewing this great eBook, please wear loose fitting shoes. *Electronic Biffytoons* will blow off your socks!

64. Electronic Rhyming Reader

Electronic Rhyming Reader might be the world's simplest and best first reader. Ideal for pre-kindergarteners, kindergarteners, Special Education students, English language learners, anyone who needs an entertaining boost into the world of literature. Each of the 40 words is illustrated by a lively cartoon, repeated frequently in entertaining patterns, and, to simplify decoding, accompanied by a rhyming word. Phonics instruction is aided with color-coding, and highlighting initial word sounds (phonemes). The PowerPoint format makes it easy to add or subtract words, creating a simpler or more complex program, whatever is best for your students. Discover for yourself if the words covered in *Electronic Rhyming Reader's* can be learned more quickly than in any other primary reader.

65. The Genius Ladder

The Genius Ladder is one our most widely used language arts programs. The eBooks is an enormous (over 500 slides!) fast paced, K-12 game for developing students' speaking and writing skills. Perfect for differentiated instruction, the program is arranged in levels from Beginner to Advanced. Play *The Genius Lad-*

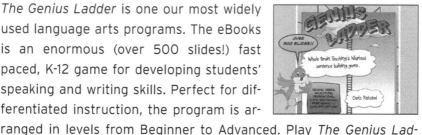

der for about 10 minutes a day and watch your kids' language skills dramatically improve. As they advance through the game, your class will learn to creatively use nouns, verbs, adjectives, prepositions, prepositional phrases, because reasoning, even appositives while writing complex topic sentences and tightly focused paragraphs. As a special bonus, *The Genius Ladder* requires no handouts or grading!

Genius Ladder Online

Webcast 504, 841
http://goo.gl/eoHeqg
http://goo.gl/FPUwFR

WBT YouTube
http://goo.gl/q3zYLO
http://goo.gl/ImJmxq
http://goo.gl/0a4rtB

The following reading games are new to this edition.

66. Musical Readers

Are your kids genuinely involved in their books during independent reading, or are they just staring at pages? Assign them reading partners, (a stronger with a weaker reader). Find a bell, flute, a musical triangle, anything that makes a pleasant noise. Every three minutes or so, gently ring the bell (or other sound maker). The kids stop and take turns, for about 30 seconds each, using lively gestures explaining their reading to their partner. Excellent use of gestures can mean positive marks on the Scoreboard (page 41) or even, if the pattern is sustained, a Super Improver star (page 31). When both partners have finished their explanations, sound the noise maker again and your students go back to reading. Using the pleasing noisemaker establishes a peaceful, reading atmosphere. When kids can perform the read/ explain routine smoothly, increase the reading time to four and then five minutes. For additional language development, ask kids to use Brainies (page 38) as they speak to their neighbor, or even as they read to themselves.

67. Musical Readers 2

Before students begin independent reading, say something like the following, "When you hear this note (use your pleasant noisemaker), please stop reading and make a prediction to your neighbor about what you think will happen next. Then give your neighbor a chance to make his or her prediction. Please use gestures to vividly make your point. Keep taking turns, making and *explaining* your prediction, until you hear this (play the note again). Then, go back to your reading, paying careful attention to see if your forcast comes true. Also, look for evidence to support your next prediction."

The same procedure can be used for helping your students make comparisons, contrasts, and connections. "When you hear the first note, compare a character in the story to another character in the same story... contrast an event in the story to another event in the story... connect something in the story to a topic we have studied in this class."

68. Adjective Mime

Using adjectives effectively is one of the simplest ways for students to make substantial improvements in their writing. Ask your kids to make the Brainy adjective gesture for each adjective they find while reading. The gesture: hold one hand over the other and then shift the top hand to the bottom and bottom hand to the top, as if you are re-shaping clay... an adjective "reshapes" a noun. As students pick up the ability to identify adjectives, the next step is to get them to appreciate them! When a student, during reading, comes to a really good adjective, lively, juicy or both... their adjective gesture should be huge.

69. Guess My Adjective

Predictably, beginning writers use the same, well-worn, adjectives over and over. Happily, students read more adjectives than they use in their compositions.

Find a story on the Internet at your students' reading level. Copy and paste the story into a word processing document. Then, before class, go through the tale and replace adjectives with strings of question marks. Thus, "sassy girl" becomes "????? girl." Pair up your students, weaker with stronger reader, and ask them to read the story replacing the ???? with as many different adjectives as possible. (Students have copies of the story, or you are using a computer projector.)

After a few minutes, call on kids to explain and defend the adjectives they chose. Then, dramatically reveal the writer's choice... guide a discussion about the effectiveness of the writer's adjectives as compared with student suggestions.

In a journal, ask kids to keep lists of their favorite adjectives and then check them off as they use them in writing.

70. Read Alouds

As you read aloud to your class, make occasional descriptive gestures. Pause occasionally and ask your kids to retell the story to each other with your, or their own, motions. As another strategy, illustrate verbs with gestures. "He *ran*... she *slept*... they *hid* under the table... " etc. Emphasize the verbs with your voice and make the appropriate movement. Kids say the verb and mirror your actions. Why? Verbs drive story action; you're keeping your students engaged by focusing on one event after another. In addition, using gestures and emphasizing key words activates your pupils' visual, auditory and motor cortices.

71. Read Aloud Desk World

As you read aloud, students listen quietly with their hands folded. Stop occasionally and say, "Desk World!" Kids walk their fingers around on their desk, imitating, and explaining, the main character's actions. If your students don't sit at desks, play *Rug World*.

72. Picture Walks

As you guide your pupils on a picture walk through a story, note the characters who appear most often. Working with your class, invent a unique gesture for each individual. The king wears a crown (gesture: put a crown on your head.) The fox is smart (gesture; tap your temple.) The monster is hungry (gesture: chomp your teeth), etc. Then, when you read aloud, make the gestures and your students mimic you. As a next step, without your prompt as you read, ask kids to make the character gestures on their own.

73. Battleships and Love Boats at the Movies

This game works wonderfully if you have feisty, argumentative kids... and who doesn't? Explain to your students, if they don't know, that books are often turned into movies. Also, explain that it is almost never the case that everything in a story makes it to the silver screen. Some scenes are deleted; other scenes are invented. The question for producers is what to keep, cut or add.

To start *Battleships and Love Boats at the Movies,* students play Paper, Rock, Scissors and the winner decides if she/he is a Battleship or a Love Boat. The Battleship is a producer who is far from thrilled about turning the story into a movie. The Love Boat is a co-producer who can't wait for production to begin.

Each pair of kids must be reading the same book. After a few minutes, ask them to stop.

The two producers have a dialogue (see below). Note that each student, Battleship or Love Boat, moves toward constructing a Triple Whammy topic sentence. After their discussion, the producers read more of the story trying to discover details that will strengthen their position. The game is played in levels; change levels as you think best. Begin by writing on the whiteboard, one of the following interchanges.

Level 1

Love Boat: This story will make a fantastic movie because _____ . (add more details)

Battleship: This story will bomb as a movie because _____ . _____ . (add more details)

Level 2

Love Boat: This movie will make millions because _____ and _____ . (add more details)

Battleship: Few people will pay to see this movie because _____ and _____ . (add more details)

Level 3

Love Boat: This movie will win an Academy Award because _____ , _____ , and _____ . (add more details)

Battleship: We should never make this movie because _____ , _____ , and _____ . (add more details)

To make *Battleships and Love Boats* even more entertaining, tell the warring producers that you play the role of The Big Banker. Make some 3x5 cards, each one labeled $1,000,000. Wander around the room, listening to the story conferences. When you like what you hear from a Love Boat, drop a few million on her. If the Battleship is making more sense, drop a few million on him. If both producers are too slow, not energetic enough, or make a mistake, transfer a million from their account to another team. If the losers complain, whisper, "Welcome to the Big Time."

74. Inviso Comics

In elementary school and sometimes in higher grades, we ask students to draw pictures illustrating events in a story. Because of the length of time involved, creating a drawing is a better art project than a literacy activity.

Inviso Comics remedies this problem.

Begin by showing your students examples of comics. Highlight the ways in which a story is framed in close ups, medium and wide angle illustrations. Encourage a discussion of the ways color, language, foreground and background details, enliven a tale. Then, hand out a sheet of paper that is divided into rectangles, like a blank comics page.

Say something like the following, "I want everyone to read carefully, looking for scenes and characters that would make a good comic. When I call out, 'Share!,' stop reading. Use the paper I gave you to make an invisible drawing that explains your reading to your neighbor. When I call out 'Read!' go back to reading, looking for more events you can illustrate."

Students can be working with the same, or different, texts. The beauty of *Inviso Comics* is that drawing imaginary pictures takes little time and builds students' abilities to visualize narrative events.

A Reading Review

For K-1 pupils, use the *Biffytoons* programs and *SuperSpeed 100* to build reading speed. Employ some of the *Read Aloud* techniques to develop student comprehension. In higher grades, move on to *SuperSpeed 1000* to increase fluency and the *Crazy Professor Reading Game* to strengthen analytical skills. For independent reading, employ variations of *Musical Readers;* add our other games when your kids are ready for new challenges.

You'll be happy to discover that some the skills your students developed in this chapter's reading contests will be powerfully effective in the upcoming math games.

CHAPTER 7

Math Games

The lottery is a tax on people who are bad at math.

— BIFFY BLUEBIRD

T he following math games are available as downloads under "Free Ebooks/general" at WholeBrainTeaching.com.

75. SuperSpeed Numbers

A lively game for school or home that teaches the counting numbers 1-100, *SuperSpeed Numbers* works like a wonder for beginning students. Players, working solo or in teams, set and break records in numerical literacy. The elegantly simple design of all the SuperSpeed games, *SuperSpeed 100, SuperSpeed 1000, SuperSpeed Letters and Phonics,* *SuperSpeed Math* and *SuperSpeed Numbers* makes them a breeze to implement. When your kids learn one program, they can play them all.

76. Smoothy Bumper Planet

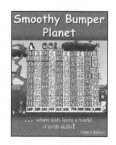

Smoothy Bumper Planet, a cartoon world, simplifies math instruction for K-2 students. Using an engaging, 3-D, color code system, kids learn to add, subtract, count to 1,000, skip count by 2s, 4s, 5s, 10s, 100s and deepen their understanding of place value for 1s, 10s, 100s and 1000s... all on the front and back of one sheet of paper! Complete instructions included for in-class or at home instruction.

77. SuperSpeed Math

Addition! Subtraction! Multiplication! Division... and a bonus section on fractions! Kids can't get enough of *SuperSpeed Math*, one of Whole Brain Teaching's most popular games. Working in pairs, one student solves as many basic math problems as possible (9 + 7 = ?, etc.) while the other student checks for correctness. In one minute rounds, players set and  break personal records. During warm ups, students spend extra time with *gnarlies*, problems that have caused them difficulty. Remarkably complete, *SuperSpeed Math* gives kids practice with every combination of numbers from 1-10 in all math operations. Because the game is oral, players receive instant feedback from their partner... and their dear teacher doesn't have to correct a problem!

> **SuperSpeed Math Online**
> Webcast 540
> http://goo.gl/YX2cgF

The following math games are new to this edition.

78. Puzzle Counting

Many kindergarteners learn to count to 100 and beyond, but have no clue what the numbers mean. If you ask a six year old, "What is 35?," you might, just might, receive the answer "35 is after 34." Using the expanded form method described below, a student would answer "35 equals 10 + 10 + 10 + 5."

When counting aloud in class, teach your kids this pattern (and gestures): "11 equals 10 + 1 (hold up 10 fingers and then 1 finger). 12 equals 10 + 2 (hold up 10 fingers and 2 fingers). 13 equals 10 + 3 (hold up 10 fingers and 3 fingers). " And so forth.

When students arrive at 20, the count becomes 20 = 10 + 10 (hold up 10 fingers twice). 21 = 10 + 10 + 1 (hold up 10 fingers twice and then 1 finger).

Once children have learned to count to 20 with expanded form, then you are ready to play *Puzzle Counting*. At random times during the day, ask the class as a whole, "What is (insert number)?" The class responds with expanded form and the matching gestures.

When *Puzzle Counting* has been mastered, go on to the following game.

79. Left Hand Place Value

Many teachers believe teaching place value is one of elementary school's most difficult, and most fundamental, lessons.

Copy and project the cartoon image of the left hand in the appendix (page 168).

Hold up your left hand, palm facing you. Beginning at your pinky finger, ask your kids to repeat the following:

"These are my little ones (baby voice: grab your left pinky finger with your right hand).

These are my big tens (child voice: grab your left ring finger).

These are my huge 100s (adult voice: grab your left middle finger).

These are my giant 1000s (giant voice: grab your left pointer finger).

And these are my GI-NORMOUS 10,000s! (huge monster, growling voice: grab your left thumb)."

After several days, when this pattern has been mastered, go on to the following steps (which make take a week or more.)

1. Teach kids to count to 9, *using a baby voice and holding onto their left pinky finger.* "1 is one little one. 2 is 2 little ones. 3 is 3 little ones." And so forth. Use counting sticks or cubes to clarify the place value of ones.
2. Teach kids to count to 20 *using a child voice and holding onto their ringer finger and then pinky finger.* "10 is one big 10 and zero 1s. 11 is one big 10 and 1 little one. 12 is one big 10 and 2 little ones." And so forth, going higher when your kids are ready.

3. After your kids learn the ten's place, go to the other fingers, 100s, 1,000s and 10,000s.

80. Help Me! Math

As your students listen to you, count forward, backward, skip count, stop anywhere, throw your hands out and exclaim, "Help me!" Your students supply, usually eagerly, the next number in the sequence.

As a variation, when your work a problem on the board, pretend to be stumped. Throw your hands out to your class, exclaim, "Help me!" Even if your kids are sometimes wrong, they will happily help their dear teacher. When you're a child, few pleasures exceed assisting a helpless adult.

81. You're Still Cool Math Facts

Similar to the above, occasionally make math mistakes on the board, some subtle, some outrageous. Teach your kids that the instant they recognize the mistake, they exclaim, "You're still cool!" and correct your error.

Next, we'll focus on games that prepare students for the Big Ordeal (Common Core or State Tests).

Now, pause again. Think back over the math games in this chapter. List the games below that will help your kids the most.

_____

_____

_____

_____

_____

_____

CHAPTER 8

Common Core/ State Test Games

I went to a public school through sixth grade, and being good at tests wasn't cool.

— BILL GATES

You've made your way through 80+ WBT games. Here's your prize. I'm going to reveal the secret to increasing student scores on Common Core and end of the year state tests. Such a simple secret. From the third week of school, kids should work on sample test questions daily. How? Turn on your grin machine, keep reading.

82. It's Raining Stars!

Odds are that your school or district has devoted many professional development days to test taking skills. The problem is, how do you motivate kids to use these skills when taking tests???

Teachers and administrators are intensely driven to improve test scores, but what's in it for students? In many states, educators can be reassigned, or lose their jobs, as a result of a pattern of low scores... but I'm a kid, I care more about Donkey Kong.

Here's our two step solution... the second step sweetens up test practice with Fun Sauce.

First, our students should be taking practice tests daily. Thousands of sample questions can be found on the Internet and the more repetitions classes receive with test taking skills, the more the skills will improve. Fifteen minutes of daily practice will increase exam competency.

Second, test prep cannot be a dreary exercise. We need *entertaining* daily test taking rehearsals.

Here's the Fun Sauce.

Your principal has identified a suite of skills, A through G, that have proven to increase student test scores. Pick one skill, A. Model the Wrong Way and the Right Way (see page 54). Ask kids to figure out why the Right Way is a Smart Choice and why the Wrong Way is a Foolish Choice. Then, your students examine a few sample questions, applying skill A. Praise kids who are the most intensely involved in practicing the skill... and give out a few Super Improver Stars (quietly draw a star on a student's test paper.) It's a long year, so be stingy in awarding stars before Christmas. Lots of reps, few stars. As the year progresses, increase the number of stars awarded during test practice.

We've never found a more motivating learning system than Super Improvers; that's why we made it Game 1. If this wonderful entertainment is part of your daily routine and kids see their classmates moving up the Super Improvers chart, any exercise that can earn stars, even practice testing, will be greeted with enthusiasm.

In a nutshell, your strategy is to practice one test skill at a time. Then, practice several skills and eventually all of them. Award Super Improver stars to individual kids, or groups, or the whole class, as you see improvement. Be stingy with the stars in the fall, a little more liberal in the winter and, in the spring... it's raining stars!

In the last few weeks before the Big Test, walk around the room with a clipboard containing the students' names. As you think appropriate, write stars next names; at the end of the practice session, transfer the stars to the Super Improvers chart.

Then, on the test day, say, "I'll be walking around watching how you're doing with my clipboard. Today is the Big Day. *I will be marking Double and Triple stars for good test taking skills!!!*"

Of course, you can't say anything to your students while they are testing... but you can carry a clipboard and silently reward their wonderful abilities.

The difficulty in preparing for, and taking, end of the year tests is that numerous skills must be mastered: core knowledge fluency, identifying key words, process of elimination. In all of the following, students work in pairs, a weaker learner with a stronger learner, before they practice the skills on their own.

83. Golden Words

Explain to your class that test writers create questions designed to fool students. One of a test writer's favorite tricks is to create questions with lots of unimportant words. You want kids to learn to dig through the Gravel, the unimportant words, that hides key information, Golden Words... the terms that lead to correct answers.

Using samples from Common Core or state tests, read questions aloud, dramatically emphasizing Golden Words. Discuss the difference between the key terms and the rest of the language, Gravel. As you pronounce each important word, clench your fists to physically express your excitement at finding Pure Gold. Make the question reading activity exciting, thrilling. *Oh, what fun to find Golden Words and beat those tricky test writers!*

Create student pairs of weaker and stronger learners. The kids take turns, reading a question, digging through Gravel, looking for Pure Gold. They repeatedly explain to each other which words are valuable. Then, ask a few students to share their discoveries. For additional effectiveness, make two copies of each test question; one for students and one to project on the whiteboard. In the second projected copy, show the Gold Words in bold face so students can evaluate the success of their digging.

84. Doofus Hunters

Pair your kids into weaker and stronger learners. Project sample multiple choice Common Core or state test questions. Each pair's task is to read a question and find the Doofus, the answer that is completely, obviously wrong. Using gestures and citing from the question, they explain to each other why the answer must be a Doofus.

Put this sentence frame on the board:

_____ is a Doofus Answer because _____ .
(add detail sentences)

Call on a few students to share their reasoning. Encourage them to add several detail sentences explaining how they came to their conclusion. Then, go on to the next question. Nothing more fun than a high energy, Doofus Hunt!

85. Trickster!

Explain (again) to your kids that test writers love to fool kids. One of a test writer's most cunning strategies is to include, in every question, answers that are incredibly close to being correct, a Trickster! Follow the same procedure as in Doofus Hunters, above. However, to build student confidence during the early stages of test preparation, include about 5-10 questions where students are hunting for a Doofus, for every question where they are looking for a Trickster.

You'll find that in order to explain why an answer is a Trickster, or a Doofus, kids will be involved in identifying the correct answer. The key to both the Doofus and Trickster exercises is to give students lots of playing time in each game. As mentioned above, we suggest that preparation for end of the year tests begin by the third week of school.

86. Secret Signs

Continue explaining the devious tricks of test writers. When they write math questions, test writers try to confuse students about the kind of math operation(s) needed to find the correct answer. Have pairs of students read lots of questions and identify whether the operations should addition, subtraction, multiplication, division or a combination. Spend considerable time playing Golden Words as preparation for Secret Signs. Pairs of students should take turns reading and discussing questions. Their task is not only to prove to each other which are the correct math operations but also why other operations are incorrect.

87. Vocabulary SuperSpeed!

Hand out list of key terms, arranged in paragraphs, that will be important during the school year and on the Big Test. List the words in the order you will introduce them in your course. Place the most important terms in bold face and/or list them several times. One student is the Speed Reader, the other student is the Mentor. The Speed Reader reads as many words as possible in one minute. The Mentor's job is to assist the Speed Reader if help is needed. At the end of the minute, the Speed Reader circles the last word read. She then, starting from the beginning, gets another chance to break her record. If the record is broken, then the next time she plays, she begins five words further from her starting point. When the Speed Reader has played twice, it's the Mentor's turn.

Understand that many key terms in your course, at any grade, are like a foreign language for your kids. They've rarely, if ever, heard words like: fraction, preposition, Gettysburg, plot, indent. The more often they rehearse these terms, as in Vocabulary SuperSpeed, the better. If they've said the word "denominator" 25 times before you introduce it in class, you won't receive puzzled looks. *Oh denominator! I've heard that word!!*

88. Prove It!

Prove it! is WBT's ultimate, test preparation game. Using whiteboards, students individually, or in pairs, select the correct answer to a projected sample test question and then prove, in writing, why their answer is correct. At a more advanced level, and requiring more time, students prove in writing why the other answers are incorrect. The previous games, excellent preparation for *Prove It!*, are rapid fire, students moving through many questions, practicing a few skills. In *Prove It!*, more time is spent with in-depth exploration. *Prove It!* is based on strategies developed at 6th Street Prep in Victorville, California, a high poverty school with some of the highest test scores in California.

89. Power Pix

It's difficult to know how students will succeed at Common Core or State Tests, if they don't understand core concepts. If a kid can't tell a verb from a noun, find the table of contents in a book, distinguish a suffix from a prefix, or perform the steps in long division, then we can hardly expect great, end of the year test scores.

To address this problem, we've created several hundred Power Pix, pictures that represent core concepts. Every Power Pix is accompanied by a lesson plan that provides a gesture, a suggested teaching schema and several assessment techniques.

Though the Power Pix were created for California standards, they address universal concepts crucial to language arts and math competency.

Here's a sample.

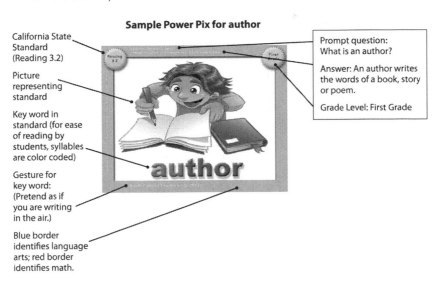

Sample Power Pix for author

California State Standard (Reading 3.2)

Picture representing standard

Key word in standard (for ease of reading by students, syllables are color coded)

Gesture for key word: (Pretend as if you are writing in the air.)

Blue border identifies language arts; red border identifies math.

Prompt question: What is an author?

Answer: An author writes the words of a book, story or poem.

Grade Level: First Grade

Power Pix are available for K-3 in math and language arts. Many third grade Pix can be adapted for higher grades.

Kindergarten: Language arts

author, black, blue, capital letter, characters, colors, end mark, exclamation mark, front cover, fiction, green, illustrator, letters, lower-case alphabet, nonfiction, orange, period, purple, question mark, red, rhyming words, sentence, setting, sorting, spaces, syllables, table of contents, title, title page, uppercase alphabet, vowels, yellow, white, word

Kindergarten: Math

addition, afternoon, big hand on a clock, calendar, circle, clock, cone, counting 1 to 5, counting 1 to 10, counting 1 to 15, counting 1 to 20, counting 1 to 25, counting 1 to 30, cube, cylinder, days of the week, equal height, equal numbers, equals sign, estimate, evening, less than, little hand on a clock, minus sign, more than, morning, noon, plus sign, pointer counting, rectangle, sorting, sphere, square, subtraction, today, tomorrow, triangle, yesterday

First Grade: Language Arts

5 W + H, apostrophe, author, capital letter, capitalized words, characters, compound word, contraction, days of the week, descriptive words, exclamation mark, illustrator, letter "I", long vowel, months of the year, noun, plot, plural noun, possessive, noun, period, prediction, pronoun, question mark, rhyming words, sentence, setting, short vowel, singular noun, title, verb, word

First Grade: Math

addition, addition checking rule, bar graph, circle, cone, counting by 2s, counting by 5s, counting by 10s, cube, dime, equals sign, estimate, foot and 12 inches, good manners, half hour, hour, left thumb rule, less than/more than, minute, nickel, nonstandard unit rule, penny, pounds and ounces, quarter, rectangle, right hand rule, sphere, square, subtraction, subtraction checking, tally marks, triangle, 1 less than, 1 more than, 10 less than, 10 more than, 1s place, 10s place, 100s place

Second Grade: Language Arts

abbreviation, adjective, alliteration, antonyms, atlas, body of a letter, cause and effect, chapter heading, characters, closing, comma, comparision, contrast, date of a letter, dictionary, draft of a paper, fact, five parts of a letter, greeting of a letter, map, noun, opinion, plot, plural noun, prefix, pronoun, proper nouns, quotation marks, rhyming words, sentence, setting, signature, suffix, syllables, synonyms, table of contents, thesaurus, verb

Second Grade: Math
addition checking rule, bar graph, cent sign, centimeter, circle, counting by 5s, counting by 10s, counting by 100s, cube, cone, cylinder, day, denominator, division, dollar, dollar sign, equals sign, estimate, expanded form, foot and 12 inches, fraction, half hour, hour, less than/ more than rule, months, multiplication, numerator equals denominator rule, nonstandard unit rule, numerator, pyramid, quarter, quarter hour, rectangle, sphere, square, subtraction checking rule, tally marks, triangle, week, year, 1s place, 10s place, 100s place, 1000s place

Third Grade: Math
3rd 1s, 10s, 100s, 1000s, 10000s place, rounding off rule, counting by 100s, counting by 1000s, expanded form, multiplication checking rule, division checking rule, multiplication, division, multiplying by zero rule, multiplying by 1 rule, dividing by 1 rule, dividing by zero rule, unit cost, total cost, unit cost rule, big slice rule, little slices rule, less than/ greater than rule, decimal point, .1, .5, .75, 1/2, 1/4, 1/3, perimeter, pentagon, hexagon, octagon, gallon, quart, pint, cup, right angle, right triangle, isosceles trriangle, equilateral triangle, parallel lines, numerator, denominator, numerator equals denominator rule, fraction, estimate, centimeter, meter, cone, cylinder, cube, square, circle, triangle, rectangle, sphere, pyramid, bar graph

Third Grade: Language Arts
alphabetical order, chapter heading, chronological order, city and state comma rule, dates comma rule, days of the week rule, draft of a paper, encyclopoedia, fact, first word of a sentence rule, geographical name rule, glossary, historical period rule, holiday name rule, homonyms, homophones, "I" rule, indented sentence, index, main idea, months rule, names of people rule, narrator, opinion, paragraph,

paraphrase, subject of a sentence, subject/verb agreement rule, topic sentence, verb tense, word family

Note Time!

Stop for a minute or two. Think back about the games you've explored. Make a list below of the ones you remember most clearly. Perhaps these are the games you should start with.

_____

_____

_____

_____

_____

_____

_____

_____

_____

_____

_____

_____

_____

_____

_____

CHAPTER 9

Challenging Kids Games

Kids don't remember what you try to teach them.
They remember what you are.

— JIM HENSON

In 1999, when my teacher friends and I began offering free seminars in Yucaipa, California, featuring new instructional techniques, we thought we knew what teachers wanted. We offered Saturday conferences on state test preparation, reading, writing, math, critical thinking. We advertised via the Internet across Southern California and never drew more than 30 educators. We pottered along, month after month, trying and failing to draw a "big crowd" (say 50 or 60 teachers).

We kept asking ourselves, "What's the Golden Key? What do we need to do to help lots of instructors?" We had no doubt, and newspaper headlines backed us up, that California, and U.S. education generally, was in serious trouble. We could see the problems, day after day, in our classrooms. My own example was that half my college students, with distressing frequency, wrote fragments instead of complete sentences, often started sentences without capitals and left off end marks. Test scores showed that my average pupil was two years behind grade level and 25% of my kids were four or more years behind. My job was to teach students who could barely read to unravel the metaphysics of Aristotle.

Then, who knows why, my colleagues and I began offering a seminar called "Teaching Challenging Kids." Boom! The Golden Key!

Within a few months our seminar attendance rocketed from 30 to 200. Over Memorial Day weekend in 2004, when administrators assured us no one would attend, we drew 500 educators to the small town of Hemet, California and turned away 400.

We believe that the problem in American education is not poor test scores or the gap between rich and poor students or the blunt fact that kids don't read much of anything except text messages. Education's problem, almost never reported in the media or analyzed in research, is that challenging kids are high-jacking our classrooms. We certainly believe no child should be left behind. We also believe that no child should be permitted to hold other children behind.

Shockingly, we've never met a teacher in years of conferences who reported that their college training adequately, or even marginally, prepared them for dealing with disruptive students. Educators enter classrooms without the skills they need to address their primary instructional problem... how to teach challenging kids.

Hopefully, you'll find time to look through *Whole Brain Teaching for Challenging Kids,* our step-by-step, classroom management guide. We're delighted that teacher reviews of our manual have given it 4.9 out of 5 stars, making it one of the highest rated books among the millions on Amazon.com.

Based on what we've said thus far, here is a yearlong plan for reforming your rebel kids and, all the while, delivering wonderfully engaging instruction to your loyalists.

1. Calculate your Classroom Engagement Average weekly (page 54). Use leadership training to move your 4s to 5s; praise 1s, 2s and 3s whenever they exhibit 4 behavior. Seat 5s, student leaders, beside your 1s, with the ultimate goal of having two student leaders for every challenging kid. Bracket the 1s with 5s on each side and, at minimum, you will insure that your Beloved Rascals will be bombarded by positive, Whole Brain, instructional energy.

2. From Day One, use the Scoreboard (see page 41). Stop scolding and start tallying positive and negative marks. Keep your kids pointed toward performing like students two grade levels higher and avoiding behavior that is two grade levels lower. Strange but true, every K-12 grade is separated by a chasm. Many fifth graders would rather go to detention than sit at a lunch table with third graders. High school sophomores, Oh so sophisticated, can be easily riled if you confuse them with eighth graders. Students dream of being older and can't stand the idea of being treated like younger kids. From a kindergartener's point of view, second graders chew tobacco and drive hot rods.

So, play on your students' passionate aspiration for upper grades and they're equally passionate aversion of behavior that might characterize lower grades. Use the Scoreboard! Tally 10-15 total marks for every hour of instruction.

3. At least by the second or third week of instruction, create a Super Improvers board (see page 32). The Scoreboard addresses class behavior; Super Improvers addresses individual behavior. The only difficulty we've found with Super Improvers is that you must change your intellectual glasses... *look for and reward improvement not excellence! Recognize growth more than ability.* As a test, after several weeks of awarding stars, inspect your Super Improver display. The highest ranking kids should not be your smartest, most polite, students... but your most improved. Assign challenging kids simple behavior goals that are within their power to reach. Give them targets they can meet. Let your Beloved Rascals feel the thrill of moving up, rising higher in the Super Improver universe.

4. Rehearse the Five Rules and the Diamond, entertainingly, many times a day. Move toward student leaders initiating rules review (page 49).

5. When the rules are well established, implement Wrong Way/Right Way practice (page 54) several times a day. When a rule is broken, use the rule call out (page 51).

After weeks of the above, go to game 89.

90. One Minute Practice

After numerous rehearsals of rules, routines, and correct procedures, it's normal to still have some kids who are holdouts. Don't scold them! Scolding, losing your temper, doesn't work... and often makes challenging kids more hostile. If a cop can arrive on a murder scene and not scold the killer, you can endure any behavior from your Beloved Rascals without losing your cool.

Try *One Minute Practice*. Explain that everyone needs to improve and that improvement is only possible through practice. Take one of your Rascals, Wild Jack, aside in the first minute of recess. Say, "I'm not angry. I just think you need to practice (insert a rule)." Jack then spends a minute silently making the rule gesture.

A minute, while the other kids are playing, feels like forever.

If Jack refuses, say, "Well, you can do it one minute my way and practice the rule. Or, you can do it two minutes your way, sit on the bench, and watch everyone else play. Which do you prefer?"

After weeks of One Minute Practice, move to *Practice Cards* (page 51). Note that each new WBT technique does not replace previous strategies. By Christmas, in a well designed WBT classroom, the instructor has a powerful set of behavior management tools: student leaders, the Scoreboard, the Super Improvers wall, Wrong Way/Right Way rehearsal, rule call outs, One Minute Practice and Practice Cards.

At any point in the above sequence, if you want a quick fix, try game 91.

91. Please-Okay La! La!

Say, "The principal has asked the teachers to work on being more polite. I'd really like to shine in this area. So, help me out! When I forget to say, 'please,' you just say 'La! La! La!' However, if I do remember to say 'please,' reward me and say, 'Okay!'" Then, practice several times a day as follows.

"Okay, we'll practice improving my manners. John, please look at me."

John says, "Okay!"

"Paulie, please sit up straight."

Paulie says, "Okay!"

"Diego, work harder!"

Diego says, "La! La! La!"

"Good job Diego. Please work harder."

Diego responds, "Okay!"

Do you see the power of the Please-Okay La La!? During your day, pretend to forget to say 'please.' Your challenging kid says "La! La! La!" You amend your request with "please!" and the Beloved Rascal says "Okay!" Wow! You never, for the life of you, have ever been able to get any Beloved Rascal to say "okay!"

As with all WBT techniques, practice and model. Not only will your manners improve, but you'll be shocked at the number of "Okays!" hidden inside your toughest kids.

And so, here's a timeline of our yearlong classroom management plan, with a central focus on reforming Beloved Rascals.

- Classroom Management Average (weekly)
- Scoreboard (from the first day: note that the Scoreboard has 10+ levels, making it yearlong game)
- Super Improvers (by the start of week three; 10 individual levels make Super Improvers longevity equal to the Scoreboard's!)
- Rule Rehearsal moving to Wrong Way/Right Way practice (by week three)
- Rule Call outs (week four)
- One Minute Practice (week 8)
- Practice Cards (after Thanksgiving)
- Please/Okay la, la (whenever necessary)

I encourage you to add the Guff Counter (stopping backtalk) and then Independents (for reforming rebel cliques) as needed to your classroom management suite. Both are described under "Levels" at WholeBrainTeaching.com.

By this point, you probably see the general strategy. Each additional technique reduces the number of challenging students and, importantly, diminishes their support among their classmates.

This brings us to our single most powerful game for improving the behavior of Beloved Rascals... The Bull's Eye Game.

92. The Bull's Eye Game

Your most challenging kids are immune to penalty and peer pressure. When you've worked through the above classroom management schedule, and still have some holdouts, you're ready for the Bull's Eye Game.

> **Bulls Eye Game Online**
> Webcast 568
> http://goo.gl/zXdANh

Follow these steps:

1. Whatever it takes, establish a talking relationship with your Beloved Rascal, Wild Jack. Praise his shoes; ask about this favorite team; listen to some of the music on his IPod. Stay at the "talking" stage for several weeks before going on to the next step.
2. Post a large, numbered bull's eye in the front of the room.

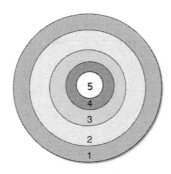

3. Take Jack aside and say that the Bull's Eye is part of a game that the two of you will play.
4. Explain that the numbers stand for student behavior. A 5 is the best behavior; a 1 is the worst behavior. Discuss and model examples of each. Wild Jack will be especially entertained when you role play him at his worst.
5. Tell your Beloved Rascal that at the end of each day, he will write down the score he thinks he earned; you will write down the score

you think he earned. If the scores match, Jack gets two points. If Jack is off by one, he gets one point. Otherwise, he scores nothing. For example, Jack had a terrible day, fighting with Leonardo on the floor. He gives himself a 1; so do you... Jack wins two points! (Why? Perhaps for the first time in his life, Jack acknowledged that he behaved terribly... a rare admission even for adults.)

6. Tell Jack that when he earns 25 points, you'll give him a prize... the only prize you've ever awarded in class. (This is why you have never given away material rewards; you save them for the ones who really need them, Beloved Rascals.) The only limit on the prize is that it can't cost more than $5.

7. At the end of every day, compare scores with Jack. When you give him a 1, ask, "What's going on at home?" This opens the door for ongoing counseling with your troubled kid.

The power of this game, as you can see, is that Jack is rewarded for honesty, taking responsibility, seeing the world from your point of view. On his worst day, Jack can still go home a winner, by matching your view of his negative behavior.

The only way this game has been conned by Beloved Rascals is when they think they can perform terribly, be honest about it, and still walk away with points. When you see this pattern say, "We're narrowing the Bull's Eye to 5-2. From here forward, whenever I think your behavior was a 1, no points for you."

In 15 years of classroom testing of the Bull's Eye Game with America's most challenging kids, teachers have reported amazing success. Time after time, often with surprising speed, defiant students have been transformed into Beloved (Former) Rascals.

93. Cussing Crusher

Sadly, more and more teachers have told me they need a way to respond to foul language. Try this: select your best, most agreeable student. Say, "I'm going to show you *exactly* what will happen if I hear profanity directed at me or anyone else. First of all, understand that

I, not you, will be the judge of foul language, words muttered under your breath... whatever. Okay, Tanya (one of your best kids). I'm going to say, 'Please work harder.' You respond, 'I'm cussing you.'"

Teacher: Please work harder.

Tanya: I'm cussing you.

Teacher; (silently pretends to fill out an office referral slip and hands it to Tanya. The key is to emphasize your response will be immediate and wordless.)

Next, say, "Okay. That's what will happen. I won't say a word. You get the office referral slip... Now, here's what will happen if you refuse to take the slip. Tanya please play your role."

Teacher: Please work harder.

Tanya: I'm cussing you.

Teacher; (silently pretends to fill out an office referral slip and hands it to Tanya. She refuses to take the slip.)

Tanya: I'm not taking that slip.

Teacher: (Silently pretends to call security)

Say, "So, if I hear foul language you get an office referral. That is the beginning of an unpleasant process for you. If you refuse to take the office referral, I call security. That leads to a longer, even more unpleasant process for you. In either case, you won't hear a word from me... but you will see my disappointed expression."

Note: if you have no faith that office personnel and/or security will follow through, backing you up, then you have a serious institutional problem. *The problem will persist until you and other teachers take whatever steps necessary to make large changes: bring the issue up at union meetings, organize school board demonstrations, invite the local news to your school... whatever it takes, you and your colleagues must be safe in your classrooms.*

Having come this far, you may wonder what remains. How about a big handful of games that don't neatly fit into any category? It's time for the Fun Factory smorgasbord.

CHAPTER 10

Assorted Wonders

If you want to build a ship,
don't drum up people together to collect wood and
don't assign them tasks and work, but rather teach them
to long for the endless immensity of the sea."

— ANTOINE DE SAINT-EXUPÉRY

94. Doo-Doo Head

A kid comes up to you at recess and says, "Jack called me a Doo-Doo head" or some other ridiculous name. You say, "Are you a Doo-Doo head?" The child says, "No." You say, "Then don't worry about it." At some point, later in the day, go talk to Jack.

I have the feeling that we are making kids too delicate, too easy to upset, too quick to tattle. If bullying is taking place, of course it needs to be stopped. Absolutely. But students need to toughen up a bit and be able to shake off minor incursions on their self-esteem.

95. Ridiculous Options

Along this same line, Jim Fay and Foster Cline, authors of *Love and Logic*, suggest that when a child comes to you with a complaint, the best strategy for building maturity and self-reliance is to say something like, "What should you do about that?"

Often the child has no clue. You respond, "Would you like me to suggest some options?" If the child agrees, and they almost always will, present several ridiculous choices. After a few moments' thought, the student will often be able to find a sensible solution. For example, Maria runs up to you and complains that Tito pushed her out of the tetherball line. Your goal as an educator is not to be the Problem Solver, but the one who nourishes your students' problem solving skills.

Your suggested options to Maria include, "Should I tell Tito that he can never, as long as he lives, play tetherball or any other game?"

"No."

"How about if we go pop all the tetherballs?"

"No."

"How about if we don't have recess for a week?"

"No."

The magic of this approach is that by wandering among absurd choices, a child often finds reasonable solutions.

96. The Pied Piper of Fun

You need a duck call. Instead of saying, "Class!" blow the duck call once and teach your kids to respond "Yes!" Two toots gets you a "Yes! Yes!" With a little practice, you can also turn the duck call into the Switch Tootler. Blow through the mouthpiece, then close your hand over the end. This produces a sound amazingly like "Uh, oh!" Your kids respond, "Uh, oh! Switch!" Best of all, with slightly more practice, your duck call becomes the Victory Trumpet. You know the sound the talented trumpeter makes at baseball games and everyone shouts, "Charge!"? You can make the same ducky version of this rousing call to action. It sounds like "toot-tittley-doo!"

When you blow the charge, your kids shout "Charge!" and immediately increase the speed and intensity of their current activity. Cleaning up? Toot-tittley-doo! "Charge!"

Summarizing a whole day's lesson with a neighbor? Toot-tittley-doo! "Charge!"

Everyone is drowsing off during your fraction lesson? Toot-tittley-doo! "Charge!"

Here's a secret. The goal of Whole Brain Teaching is to turn you into the Pied Piper of Fun, a sweet tootler who kids will follow anywhere... even across arid Homework Desert, even up Mount Fraction, even down into Test Prep Chasm.

Brain Fact:

The brain's least reliable memories are acquired through the auditory cortex. Listening to lecture may be the worst way for the brain to learn. You sat through 100s of hours of college lectures. Given the way your brain works, don't be astonished if you remember so little. As we say in WBT, the longer you talk, the less your kids learn.

---

97. Two Finger Action Figures

Your students will be delighted to learn that they have a toy growing from each palm. Walk two fingers around in the air, then up and down piles of books, then across a map. Show your students the wondrous adventures possible with Two Finger Action Figures. Start by telling your kids to use their new toys in Desk World (see below) to retrace the action in a story. Other Two Finger Action Figure activities include: synching finger steps to adding and subtracting ("Make a dot on your desk. Walk forward five steps, walk back three steps, how many steps are you from the dot?"), marching off inches on a foot ruler, pacing across dates on a timeline, demonstrating wise and foolish behavior around the Invisible Miniature Jungle Gym floating in the air in front of each student. And so forth.

98. Anti-Gravity Boots

Long criticized by the Gloom Society as "being way too much fun," Anti-Gravity Boots are the perfect apparel for Two Finger Action Figures.

Watch what happens when Action Figures march up Arm World (see below) retelling a story and using their Anti-Gravity Boots to leap amazingly high at the most exciting parts. Tell your neighbor the four steps in the math problem and get those Action Figures leaping up, up, up the Dark Mountain of Step Four. Whenever you are proofreading and find an error in your paper, activate the Anti-Gravity Boots and quietly jump your Two Finger Action Figure up and down once. And so forth.

99. Desk World

A desktop can be anywhere. Show your kids a map of Marco Polo's journey to China. Point out key locations on his travels. Then, tell them to trace out those places on Desk World, recounting the great explorer's adventures. Or, after a science lesson, ask kids to draw an invisible picture of the human circulatory system on Desk World. Trace the blood flow from the heart, through the main arteries, all the way down to the capillaries in the legs (at the bottom of Desk World). Desk World is a great place for Two Finger Action Figures to play with Pencil-Bots (see below)… when they're not marching up and down Arm World.

100. Arm World

An arm, held out horizontally, can represent any length of time. The fingertips stand for the beginning of the time period and the shoulder is the time period's end. For example, students can point to locations on their arm and retell a story, from the opening (finger tips) to the end (shoulder). Or, Arm World can represent steps in a science experiment. First, put on your goggles (fingertips). Then, open your lab manual to page 42 (palm). Next, very carefully, light the Bunsen burner (fingers slowly slide up to the elbow)… and so forth.

Long chronological sequences can be represented by going up one arm, over the top of the head, and down the other arm. The Ice Ages begin on the left hand. The top of the head is the Renaissance. Way down here on the tippy tip of the right fingers… that's when we invented video games. Obviously, Arm World is a merry place for Two Finger Action Figures.

101. Logic Cliff Bungee Jumper

The most difficult, and crucial, task in writing Triple Whammy sentences (page 91) is finding three strong pieces of evidence to support the initial statement. Here are examples of the two most common student errors:

I love Whole Brain Teaching because it is fun, entertaining, and free. The problem is that "fun" and "entertaining" overlap. Thus, they could not be expanded into two separate paragraphs in the body of an essay.

I love Whole Brain Teaching because it is fun, free, and used by everyone around the world. Now, we have three, non-overlapping reasons... but unfortunately, the third piece of evidence is false. Thus, it should not be developed as a paragraph in an essay.

When students construct Triple Whammies the most frequent errors will be overlapping evidence, like the first one above or evidence that doesn't support the initial statement, like the second one above. Using your computer projector or a whiteboard, show your pupils lists of correct and incorrect Triple Whammy statements. Read them slowly. The kids hold out their arms with one hand as a Two Finger Action Figure "standing" on the back of the other hand. When you read an incorrect statement, everyone's Action Figure bungee jumps into the air, singing, "Aiiiii" and then, because of the elastic bungee cord, bounces back to the back of the hand. The bungee jump symbolizes a Triple Whammy that "jumped off topic." The return signals a chance for students to make a correction.

Once pupils understand the types of problems that can cause a Triple Whammy to leap off topic, ask them to construct and share their own correctly and incorrectly constructed Triple Whammies.

102. The Pencil Bot

A pencil can be anything. Look, my pencil is light ray, speeding from the moon to the earth, in only 1.3 seconds. Goodness, my pencil is the Nile River, the longest in Africa. The eraser is the headwaters of the Nile at Lake Tanganyika and the point is where the Nile floods past Alexandria into the Mediterranean. Now my pencil is a sloping line. You remember last week how we calculated slopes for various lines? Use your Pencil Bot and explain the formula to your neighbor.

Of course, the Pencil Bot can only be activated by tapping it once on the eraser and whispering the magic word, "kkkxlxmopwurfdoogle."

103. Rat-a-tat Pointers

Sometimes you need your class to read information off the board, or from a projected slide. You want to be sure that everyone is focused in the right direction. Tell your kids, "So that I know you are really paying attention to our lesson, waggle the forefinger of each hand at the whiteboard, as you read." When you see kids not rat-a-tatting, go over to them and whisper, "thank you for demonstrating Wrong Way rat-a-tatting. Now, show me Right Way rat-a-tatting."

104. Paper Thumper

You've asked your kids to read key information from a handout, or book. Guess what? Some of your Beloved Rascals may not follow your directions! To make reading more entertaining, and thus more engaging, tell your students to thump on key points. Using your imagination, demonstrate marvelous two grade level higher thumping and miserable two grade lower thumping. *Hey, my friends! Let's thump like big kids!*

105. Precise Pointy Fingers

When you use your Attention Getter and say, "Class!" Your kids, with rehearsal, will respond, "Yes!" and fold their hands. To discover, as you have all through these games, how many students will be enthralled by On Task Silliness, ask your kids to use Precise Pointy Fingers. Their extended forefingers point at you wherever you go. (To make Precise Pointy Fingers, fold your hands; then, extend your forefingers so the tips are touching. Pretend like you are a student; your forefingers move from side to side, flawlessly indicating the wandering teacher's location.)

106. The Step-Step-Steppers

At every grade level, there are numerous lessons where we want students to follow a sequence of steps. Writing, math, science experiments, cleaning up, art activities all involve multiple stages. Set up a row of empty chairs, desks, books on the floor, anything physical and moveable. Stand behind the first item and say, "The first step will be…" Then, move to the second item, 'The second step will be…" and so forth. If one stage is more important than another, say, "Note that I have (turned the chair upside down…. opened the book… whatever). This means you have to be careful at step four because…." After you've finished explaining a few stages, ask the kids to teach each other what you said. Walk around the room, check comprehension and then, as appropriate, review previous steps or describe new ones.

107. Classroom Compass

An engaging way to teach complex geography lessons is to draw a compass on a large sheet of paper with North, South, East and West noted on the four edges. Place the Classroom Compass on the floor in the middle of your room. If you are teaching a lesson on American history, your kids are then divided into four regions, Northerners, Southerners, Easterners, and Westerners. Talk about various migrations, important events, conflicting interests among the various areas of the U.S. Or, if the lesson is on state history, use the four regions to discuss natural resources, historical events, important cities… whatever your lesson requires. Or, link various areas of the classroom to the projection of a map. "Juan, and the other kids in the corner are the Northeast; Sandy and her row are the Eastern seaboard; down here, where I'm standing, is New Orleans … point at each place in our classroom and tell your neighbor the map location." Best of all, hand out a state or national map with your school's location marked. Describe the surrounding locales. Take your class outside, maps in hand.

Look! Someone has chalked a compass on the playground!

Ask your kids to talk about what they would see, if they travelled from their current location in each of the four compass directions.

108. Crack Up City

As a Scoreboard tweak, tell your pupils that when they end up with three more positive than negative marks on the Scoreboard, they win a trip to Crack Up City. Tell them to come prepared the next day with several short, corny jokes they have copied from the Internet... or heard from Wacky Old Grandpa. Don't let the class win for a few days. Then, before dismissal, have selected kids, everyone wants to be chosen, read a few jokes. Crack Up City is even more entertaining if you crank up the Laugh Machine.

109. The Laugh Machine

When class is dragging, for example, late in the day, let your kids crank up their Laugh Machines (LM). As if there is a handle sticking out of their heads, your students turn a few cranks in the air, firing up their LMs. When you lift your hands, making a face like the funniest clown on earth, the kids laugh uproariously. When you bring your hands down, they instantly stop. Spend some time Laugh Machine practicing. Then, start your lesson. "Right now, we're going to review three kinds of rocks. It's going to be so much fun (Laugh machine on... Laugh Machine off)! You'd never guess it but all rocks we studied are really hard (Laugh machine on... Laugh Machine off). Remember that igneous rocks come from volcanoes. In the old days, volcanoes spewed lava (Laugh machine on... Laugh Machine off). They still do (Laugh machine on... Laugh Machine off)." And so forth.

It's best to activate Laugh Machines right before dismissal. Your kids' pretend laughing becomes real laughing becomes time to go.

The Laugh Machine works best if you're a Corny Teacher. If Corny jokes don't come naturally, you haven't been in education long enough. See your doctor and ask for a giggler transplant.

110. Wacky Animal Fun Button

Draw a large red circle on the board; this is the Wacky Animal Fun Button. Whenever the button is "pushed," touched by a finger, the kids make Wacky Animal noises, until the finger "releases" the button.

Then, your students instantly fall silent. Practice a few times. Then say, "If we work hard, right before recess, whoever is doing a great job, can press the *Wacky Animal Fun Button!*" Kids love to control kids. Challenging kids, especially, love to be the comic master of ceremonies.

111. Leader Spotlight

We are often asked at conferences what should be done about kids who don't go along with one or more Whole Brain Teaching techniques. We suggest Leader Spotlight. Whenever you wish, have an in class rehearsal of a WBT strategy: Class-Yes, Mirror Words, Teach-Okay, or one of the Five Rules. Ask a few of your leaders to stand up and mix in a Rebel, Sassy Sarah. Of course, you won't point out who is who.

Say, "I'm interested in how this group will do as classroom leaders." Then, ask the group to demonstrate the Wrong Way to demonstrate a WBT technique. What's Sassy going to do? Even if she does nothing, Sassy is still demonstrating the Wrong Way! Next, stand next to her; ask the leader group to demonstrate the Right Way to perform the WBT technique. With only a few kids standing, there is nowhere for your Rebel to hide. Even if Sassy is uninvolved, her brain is mirroring the activity surrounding her. Rebel outside, Loyalist inside!

112. Scoreboard Dice

After you have progressed far into the year and ascended many levels of the Scoreboard, dice and a element of chance can be introduced to fire up student enthusiasm. Dice are rolled at the end of the day when Smilies outnumber Frownies. If you are playing boys versus girls, then dice are only rolled if both sides finish with more positive than negative points. Here is a suggested schedule for dice roll bonuses:

- Snake eyes: Dice roll 2: no reward!
- Dice roll 3-6: everyone wins one minute more recess.
- Dice roll 7-10: everyone wins five minutes of free reading time.
- Dice roll 11-1:2 everyone wins one page less homework

113. The Real Brain Game

Teach your kids the following, with gestures.
- The pre-frontal cortex controls reasoning (tap the middle of your forehead).
- The motor cortex controls movement (tap the top of your head).
- The visual cortex controls seeing (tap the rear of your head).
- The auditory cortex controls speaking and hearing language (tap the left side of your head).
- The limbic system controls memory creation and emotions (Point one finger from each hand into the left and right side of your head, as indicating an area deep inside the brain... the location of the limbic system).

Explain that lecture only activates part of the auditory cortex, the listening region in the auditory cortex. This is why lecture is so boring... it's Teensy-Brain Learning. Then, explain why, in WBT, we use so many gestures and visual cues, speaking and hearing, emotion activation. This is Whole Brain Learning. When the entire brain is involved in a lesson, it's impossible to be bored. You have no mental area left over to think about the clock.

Then, during lessons make Mirror Words remarks like, "Motor cortex activate! I want to see big, motor cortex gestures... Visual cortex activate... all eyes on me!... Auditory cortex activate!... listen and repeat this lesson... Prefrontal cortex activate! Start planning with your neighbor how to solve these math story problems!... Limbic system activate! Crank up those memory creating gestures and emotions!"

114. Victory Poses

Amazingly enough, research indicates that when we assume a victory pose, arms up the air or proudly on our hips, our neurochemistry changes. When we hold a victory pose for two minutes, our brains produce more dopamine, a pleasure inducing chemical, and less cortisol, a neurotransmitter associated with depression. *Your body language alters your brain chemistry!* The worst thing to do when you feel bad is slump over dejectedly. Dejected slumping pumps blues juice into your brain. An alternative when feeling rotten? Do the Yippee Polka.

When several students show significant improvement in academic or social skills, ask everyone to stand and mirror a victory pose of the students' (or your) choice. Let spontaneous cheering erupt (warn your neighbors). For an extra boost, play the theme music from Rocky or "We are the champions." Happy bodies, happy kids. Don't celebrate for longer than 10-15 seconds... or you will have to scold your students for excessive merriment.

Note: there is a wonderful YouTube video showing a group of soldiers in Africa laughing at a chimp. The chimp picks up a rifle, the soldiers laugh a bit harder and then, realizing their danger, stop. The chimp starts firing. The soldiers dive into the bushes. What does the chimp do? Drops the rifle. Jumps up and down. Thrusts its hairy arms upward into, you guessed it, a Victory Pose! Humans lose! Apes win! Yea!

115. Mind Giants

(Free download under "Free Ebooks/general" at WholeBrainTeaching.com)

Do your kids need critical thinking help in Math? Literature? Common Core? Writing? State standards? Social studies? History? Mind Giants to the rescue! Biffy Bluebird helps kids create great questions; Smarty Wonderbeak supplies amazing answers; Big Dilly, such a wise fellow, always wants more details; Dilly Dilly guides thoughtful analysis with Who? What? Where? When? Why? How? Your kids will love using the lively Mind Giant cartoon characters as insightful allies in any task requiring careful thought. Watch in delight as the Mind Giants help your students pose insightful questions, support generalizations with examples, answer questions with text quotations, strengthen arguments with robust evidence, utilize academic vocabulary, transform a deep thinking exercise into an energetic, thought provoking romp.

116. Disguise Cream

The special power of Disguise Cream is that when you rub it anywhere on your skin, you become whatever you're thinking about. Disguise Cream can turn a class into polar bears to explore their North Pole habitat. Or, Disguise Cream, could turn pairs of kids into numerators and denominators. The numerators would describe what it means to be a numerator; the denominator would describe what it means to be a denominator. Of course, they would argue about who was most important in a fraction. An entire class could coat itself in Disguise Cream and become Navajos or their favorite character from a story or, even, magically transform themselves into college professors, demonstrating remarkably well mannered, lunchroom behavior.

117. Wonder Goggles

In Whole Brain Teaching, we believe every lesson's highest goal is to show students the Wonder of what they are learning. The problem, and the glory, of education's Wonders is that each one is unique. The Wonder of fractions is different than the alphabet's Wonder. Thus, we can give you no universal solution to the problem of teaching Wonders. However, here are four examples. (You may disagree and discover unique Wonders of your own.)

- The Wonder of Numbers is that so few of them, only ten symbols, 0-9, can create an infinite number of combinations. The symbols can represent a number smaller than the smallest atom or larger than the largest galaxy. At the bottom of the sea, the ocean's depth can be expressed in numbers. The length of a gnat's nose can be stated in a number. The quantity of hairs in a square inch of a cat's fur (100,000!) can be expressed as a number. To teach the Wonder of numbers find amazing numerical facts, like the little patch of cat's fur, to stun your kids into amazement.
- The Wonder of Blue is that so many different kinds of things can be blue: the sky, a Christmas ornament, a lake, a cold nose,

a blueberry. A key to teaching the Wonder of a color is to encourage kids to name as many different kinds of things that are naturally that color... and things that are rarely, perhaps never, that color. There are an infinite number of things that are blue and a much larger infinity of things that are not blue.

- The Wonder of Infinity is that it is one of the few concepts that we can talk about but never understand. We can talk about railroad tracks that extend into infinity, but we can't understand what that means. We can visualize "ending" not "never ending." As soon as we visualize "never ending" railroad tracks, we see where they end.

- The Wonder of Talking is that you learn to talk without ever thinking about learning to talk. Once you can talk, if you think about everything your mouth and tongue have to do, you can't talk! As soon as you try to describe how you talk, you make talking impossible. What would you have to say to someone to teach her all the mouth and tongue movements involved in reading this sentence? Talking is something we can do easily but is impossible to describe how we do it!

To make Wonder Instruction deeply engaging, tell your students to put on their custom fitted Wonder Goggles. With this special pair of glasses, kids can see, and think about, a Wonder whenever you investigate it... and, even better, begin to look for their own Wonders.

118. Improvement Slogans

As I've mentioned a number to times, our single goal in Whole Brain Teaching is to reward for improvement. We may praise excellent work, but we save our highest praise for improved work. We reward for a good job, but a bigger reward is for a better job. We want to create learning environments where students strive to break personal records. Here are a few Improvement Slogans that can be posted around the room... but don't reveal them all at once. To create suspense, start with the posters face to the wall, and then turn them around rewards for doing well on one of the previous 118 games.

- Dream Bigger.
- Work Harder. Be Nicer.
- Want a Smiley? Be a Smiley.
- Smash! Pulverize! Shatter!... a PR today. (Put up this sign so kids will ask, "What's a PR?" You reply, "A Personal Record. Which PR will you Smash, Pulverize, Shatter today?"
- Improve Astonishingly.
- Victory for One. Triumph for All. (Explain that when one student improves, everyone receives credit because the whole class is creating a positive, hard working atmosphere.)
- Learning is a team sport.
- Inspire everyone.
- Got improvement? Prove it!

119. Grit

Assume you are rich scientist who loves educational experiments. You form a school of 1,000 kids. There are three groups: rich kids who are not terribly smart and don't have much perseverance, smart kids who are not terribly rich and don't have much perseverance, persevering kids who aren't terribly rich or smart. Ten years later you assess which kids grew up to be successful at life. Which group had the lowest rates of depression, the fewest divorces, the highest paying jobs, the best health. Recent research indicates that perseverance, grit, is the best predictor of adult well being.

The top 10 hits on a Google search on "grit research" include: National Geographic, Forbes, National Public Radio, the Association of Psychological Science, the University of Pennsylvania School or Arts and Sciences and a TED talk.

Persevering, gritty kids win life's race.

So, how do we teach perseverance or grit?

Reward grit with a special, gold star on the Super Improvers Team. These special stars have a blank at the center where you can write

2, 3, 4, or 5. The golden grit award is your classroom's highest treasure because it's worth from 2-5 regular Super Improver stars. Kids can display perseverance in completing test taking, math tasks, essays, science experiments, art exercises, computer learning games. A little improvement in grit, determination, stick-to-it-iveness... that's a two point grit star. An amazing amount of improvement in grit... wow! That's a five point grit star. *We should reward grit in any activity where a child might normally be expected to quit.*

Of every gritty challenge in WBT, I believe none is more praiseworthy than the use of the Detail Adder Brainy.

120. Detail Adder Brainy Grit

We always want kids to say more, give additional information, supply extended thoughtful details. The most frequent remark I wrote on my college students' papers was "More!"

If you explore *The Brainy Game* under Free Ebooks at WholeBrainTeaching.com, you'll find a description of Detail Adders. When a student answers a question in class, roll your forefingers around each other and say, "Tell me more!" Every other student should mimic your Detail Adder gesture and repeat your words.

It's time for a Detail Adder, Tell me more!, whenever a pupil uses any of the following Brainies: because, for example, also, if-then, or creates Brainy simile, metaphor, comparison or contrast. When students provide Detail Adders, adding additional, relevant information, they are engaged in a crucial, critical thinking task: expanding simple statements into complex, multi-part insights.

As students persevere in Detail Adders and move from speaking sentences to speaking paragraphs, they are taking one of the most significant leaps in education. Reward them with a Grit Star, maybe even a 5 pointer, on the Super Improver Wall.

Do you have the feeling that I saved the best games for last, Growth Talk and The Brain Tree? I did. Almost. Unless you're a newbie teacher with a class of gang bangers. Read on.

121. Growth Talk

As teachers and parents, we naturally want to increase kids' self es-teem. However, recent research by Stanford's Carol Dweck, and oth-ers, indicates that increasing students' self esteem often does not im-prove academic performance. If we say, "you're great... wonderful... fantastic... incredible" pupils frequently have no reason for increasing effort; too often they avoid academic challenges because this might make them less than "great." Dwek constrasts a Fixed Mindset class-room (praising for ability) with a Growth Mindset classroom (prais-ing for improvement, effort, grit). In WBT, we use Growth Talk. We want kids to understand that their brains grow, that intelligence is not fixed, that ability, through effort, improves. Thus, during Teach-Okay, we stress "larger gestures, more energy, grow your brain!" On the Scoreboard, we continuously point out that students should use two grade levels higher as their improvement target. We praise increased speed and energy in responding to the Five Rules. The Super Improv-ers Team explicitly rewards improvement rather than ability. As you will see, game 122, The Brain Tree, our implementation strategy, is framed by a growth metaphor.

The brain and Growth Talk: There may be no more powerful benefit for students than teaching them that their brains can grow. Dweck's research demonstrates that pupils, even the best, with a Fixed Mind-set often decline in academic ability because they have no investment in overcoming challenges. Students with a Growth Mindset are eager for new tasks, enjoy effort, see themselves on a path of continuous improvement... which is exactly what we want!

Why should we use Growth Talk?

- Students who believe their ability is fixed avoid challenges and exhibit what has been termed "learned helplessness."
- Students with a Growth Mindset understand the true nature of their brains, a "muscle" that grows through challenging exercise.

Do: Frequently point out that it is effort, more than ability, that leads to life success. Use examples of successful individuals in sports, movies, business ... and your own personal experience. Praise effort, "you really worked hard on this"... "this part of the essay shows the most slow, careful focus"... "I see that you are putting everything you've got into this drawing"... "look at how much you have learned in math... keep growing!"... "your leadership skills are developing"... "you are using more energy teaching your neighbor."

Do post Growth mottos (great for classroom banners!): "The more we know, the more our brains grow." "Hard lessons are dandy Brain Candy." "We can break any record we set." "There are no shortcuts to excellence." "The more effort, the more success." "Every forest can grow more trees. Every tree can grow more leaves. We are the forest of those trees." (Make a large sign with the word Can't in a circle crossed out by a red line, signaling that we never say Can't). "Kick the Can't!" "Know to Grow!"

Do grow sweet potatoes!: Kids need a visual example of dramatic growth. Put sweet potatoes in jars of water around the room. Encourage discussion of which plants will grow the fastest ... and how brain growth is exemplified by the sweet potatoes.

Don't: praise intelligence, "you're really smart... intelligent... bright... gifted."

122. Implementing WBT: The Brain Tree

Here are some of the key strategies we have discussed: Class-Yes, Five Rules, Hands & Eyes, Mirror Words, Teach-Okay, Switch, The Scoreboard, Super Improver, and just now, Growth Talk. How should they, and any of our other entertainments, be implemented? Like everything else in WBT, turn implementation into a game. Decide which, and how many, strategies you want to begin with. Add about one new technique per week. At the end of each week, ask your kids to assign a score of 1-3 leaves (points), assessing how well the class (teacher and students) grew in each strategy. To increase your students' engagement, post the Brain Tree grid on your classroom door. Even better, if you are artsy, create a large tree with bare branches on your door. Add a cut out or drawn leaf for every new point scored. Let other students and teachers wonder at your students' achievements and compare their growth to yours.

Note: fill in the grid starting in the lower left corner, so, week by week, the grid becomes a "growing" bar graph.

SAMPLE **Brain Tree**	Week 1	Week 2	Week 3	Week 4	Week 5	Week 6	Week 7	Week 8
Growth Talk								
Super Improver								
Scoreboard								
Switch								
Teach-Okay								
Five Rules								
Mirror Words								
Hands & Eyes								
Class-Yes								
TOTAL LEAVES								

1 leaf = 1 point
2 leaves = 2 points
3 leaves = 3 points

(See sample Brain Tree grid below; fill in leaves from bottom to top, so the grid shows upward growth.)

SAMPLE	Week 1	Week 2	Week 3	Week 4	Week 5	Week 6	Week 7	Week 8
Growth Talk								
Super Improver								
Scoreboard								
Switch							3	
Teach-Okay					2	2	3	
Five Rules					1	1	2	
Mirror Words			1	3	3	2	3	
Hands & Eyes	2	3	3	3	3	2	2	
Class-Yes	1	3	3	3	3	1	3	
TOTAL LEAVES	3	6	7	9	12	11	13	

Brain Tree

Here is a sample of the first seven weeks of the Brain Tree game. Note that whatever techniques introduced are maintained throughout the game. The instructor decides when a new strategy should be implemented. The above order of strategies, in general, moves from easiest to most challenging... but any order may be selected by the instructor. Week six above is a crucial week; scores declined in several categories. Thus, the teacher decided to not introduce new techniques in week 7... and postponed work on the Switch introduced in week six.

Brain Tree Scoring

At the end of each week, your class awards itself 1 to 3 leaves for each strategy you have decided to implement. A rubric for lower (1) and upper (3) scores is presented below. Encourage discussion of the "middle" score, 2 leaves. To boost scores, frequently (5 times per day if necessary) rehearse lower and then higher performance. "Show me a Class-Yes 1 point." "Great! Now show me Class-Yes 3 points." Rehearsals need not take more than a minute. For brain growth, frequency of rehearsals is more important than length. Begin with any strategies you wish; add others as needed. The nine techniques below form a solid instructional foundation.

Class-Yes
1 leaf = students rarely respond quickly with "yes" or with hands folded.

3 leaves = almost all students respond quickly with "yes" and hands folded.

Hands and Eyes
1 leaf = students rarely respond quickly with "hands and eyes" and hands folded.

3 leaves = almost all students respond quickly with "hands and eyes" and hands folded.

Mirror Words
1 leaf = students rarely imitate the teacher's gestures and words.

3 leaves = almost all students imitate the teacher's gestures and words.

Five Rules
1 leaf = When a rule is called out, for example, "Rule 1", few students respond rapidly with "Follow directions quickly" or demonstrate the gesture.

3 leaves = Almost all students respond rapidly and use gestures during rule callouts.

Teach Okay

1 leaf = The teacher delivers lessons that are too long for students to repeat to each other. Few, if any, students make a full turn or use gestures when teaching neighbors.

3 leaves = The teacher's lessons rarely exceed 2-4 sentences. Almost all students make a full turn and use gestures when teaching neighbors.

Switch

1 leaf = Few students respond energetically to the Switch request.

5 points = Almost all students respond energetically to the Switch request.

Scoreboard

1 leaf = The teacher marks fewer than five total marks, positive plus negative, per hour of instruction. Few, if any, students respond quickly with a Mighty Oh Yeah or Mighty Groan.

3 leaves = The teacher marks a minimum of 15 total marks, positive plus negative, per hour of instruction. Almost all students respond quickly with a Mighty Oh Yeah or Mighty Groan.

Super Improver

1 leaf = The teacher rarely talks about, or recognizes, student improvement. One or two stars are awarded per day. Students exhibit little enthusiasm for ascending in rank on the Super Improvement Team.

3 leaves = The teacher frequently talks about, and recognizes, student improvement. Four or more stars are awarded per day. Students exhibit lively enthusiasm for ascending in rank on the Super Improver Team.

Growth Talk

1 leaf = The teacher rarely talks about brain growth or recognizes student improvement. Students are praised much more often for ability, "good work," than effort.

3 leaves = The teacher frequently talks about brain growth and recognizes student improvement, especially in effort.

As you may be able to tell, *The Brain Tree* solves many teaching problems. Here are answers to questions that I imagine you asking.

Problem: With 122 games to choose from, how should I begin?
Answer: Start with some of the top 10 games described in chapter 3; list them on your Brain Tree in the order that seems easiest to implement. Or, simply start with the nine strategies I've listed on the sample Brain Tree diagram.

Problem: How do I know if I'm successful?
Answer: Leave evaluation of implementation up to your kids... the resident experts on how much they are learning!

Problem: When should I add a new technique?
Answer: Add new techniques when your students frequently self-score 2-3 points on established strategies.

Problem: What about teachers who don't go along with Whole Brain Teaching?
Answer: Invite them to post their own Brain Tree, listing non-WBT strategies they want to "grow." How you improve instruction is negotiable... that you must continuously improve your teaching is non-negotiable.

Problem: What if I forget to use the Brain Tree?
Answer: All you have to do is post the grid (and artsy tree!) on your classroom door... your kids, eager to see how many leaves they're earning in comparison to other classes, will remind you.

CHAPTER 11

Rookie Teacher at Nightmare High

You can't direct the wind, but you can adjust the sails.

— THOMAS S. MONSON

Secondary teachers are a tough crowd. During conferences, I've stared into hundreds of skeptical faces. Middle school and high school instructors often have the view that there is nothing WBT, or any other system, can offer that will win over resistant teenagers.

So, I ask my doubtful audience to perform a thought experiment. You're a new teacher. You've got a class of gang bangers.

I invite them to talk to each other about what they will do on the first day. Usually the response is head scratching or the unhappy laughter of despairing educators.

After a bit of discussion, I offer the plan described in this chapter.

After I talked at conferences for a year or so about the rookie teacher at Nightmare High, I realized our methods would not only work for any rowdy grade... but also, many features might be useful in a class of angels.

So, imagine you're sitting in my audience.

You're a rookie at the worst school in the district. Of course, you get the toughest kids, a class of 35 gang bangers. The newbie teacher is always thrown into the deep end.

The support staff is haggard, dazed, crunched in the middle and burnt on both ends... the poor battered souls would greet the Apocalypse as good news.

You search for colleagues who are ramrods, take charge ring masters, but the teachers' lounge is filled with educators who are frothy whips of Jell-O and pabulum.

What should you do?

The first thing to realize, and it is wonderful, is that you have a free hand. You've got the class no one wants and that everyone thinks is unteachable.

When you and your kids are expected to fail, you've got nothing to lose.

Shoot for the moon.

The second thing to realize is that your class is not, no matter how it appears, 35 against one. Every group of rebellious teens breeds a nucleus of leaders.

It's you, with a free hand, against the few.

Dear Colleague: get the leaders on your side and you might make it to your first paycheck.

The third thing to realize, and let this sink in, is that you have no power. Don't go into class and exercise authority you don't possess. You're in the cage with the big cats. Crack a whip and they'll be picking their teeth with your shin bones.

Again. You have no power.

The only assignment your Rascals will complete is one that doesn't look like an assignment. You have to find leaders, so start your kids talking about birthday parties (see page 57). Explain that you are *thinking about* creating a seating chart and *might* want to seat close friends together. Don't commit to seating friends together... it's your ace in the hole. Don't worry about profanity, hand raising, just keep the talk flowing about birthday parties.

Here's a general rule with the toughest classes. If you have something rebel kids want, don't give it to them right away. They want to be seated with their friends. Don't dish out this reward, until you have other motivational prizes to offer.

After some free flowing talk (on the subject *you* picked... point for the you!) wrap up the Birthday Game as follows, "First thing I need to know, is who can follow directions. Those are the students who might be mature enough for focused work, even though they are seated next to friends. So, please, quickly, list the names of three kids in this class who you would invite to your birthday party."

You have five classes, all wooly with rebellion. Should you play the Birthday Game with every class or only your most agreeable? The wildcats with the smallest teeth.

You're in a hostile habitat where you have no power, but ample freedom. Your goal is to use the natural tendencies of the populace for their own improvement. Teens have leaders; so you must organize the leaders. They like birthday parties; so you talk about birthday parties. Teens feverishly text each other... so use social media to your advantage. Play the Birthday Game with one class, mention seating charts and, without fail, kids will text this information to their friends.

The next day, your other classes will demand to know why they were cut out of the fun. Don't faint. They want into your game (another point for you!). Say, "When I see some progress in this class, like everyone looking at me when I'm teaching, I'll be happy to talk about birthdays and seating charts. Let's see how today goes... tell your neighbor, hey! If Period 4 gets to play a game, so should we!"

My own advice is to play the Birthday Game with the least rowdy of the rowdies. Always solve the easiest problems first.

Okay. You have the names from one class (add other classes, at your pleasure). Write every student's name on a large sheet of paper. If Tito invites Laura to his birthday party, draw an arrow from Tito to Laura. If Laura invites Winnie, draw an arrow from Laura to Winnie. When you're finished... contemplate the wonder you've created.

Arrows here, there, crisscrossing, avoiding some kids, making others look like pin cushions... pincushions of popularity. *You are staring at a map of the subterranean social structure of your rebels.*

You see the Insiders and Outsiders. You have information your kids prefer to hide. The most popular students, the pincushions, would never be so uncool as to proclaim their popularity. Claiming you're cool is uncool. Your leaders hoard power, especially from a geek like their teacher.

Go in the next day and hold a discussion about Good Leaders and Bad Leaders. Explain that leaders could be classmate, bosses, teachers, parents, coaches, etc. Hand a sheet of paper and pencil to a popular kid; ask her to make a list of the characteristics of good and bad leadership as mentioned by the class. You'll be delighted to see that you and your gang bangers are on the same moral planet. In essence, good leaders help others and bad leaders help themselves (and harm others). You and your kids agree! Don't make a big deal out of this, but inwardly cherish the moment.

On the next day, you can't move too quickly with a class of Beloved Rascals, display the list of characteristics of Good Leaders. Say something like the following, "An important part of this class, because I think you are old enough, will be leadership training. Look at your list of positive leadership characteristics. Write down the names of 4-7 classmates who you think would make good leaders."

Names are written down. Don't try to discourage bantering... remember you don't have any power (yet).

Take the list of names home and compare them to the results of the Birthday Game. Request input from staff who know your kids. Make your best selection of pincushion kids and other students who veteran teachers convince you would be sound candidates for leadership training.

On the next day, your world changes.

Go into class with a list of leaders. Everyone, especially the leaders!, wants to know the names on the list. Let me emphasize this point. You have something all your kids, especially the pincushions, want... *who are those leaders? Did anyone pick me? Is my best friend in? Oh no, is my worst enemy in???*

Say something like the following at the start of the period, "I have the list of leaders here. If we work hard, maybe at the end of the hour we'll have time to announce them." Remember. If you have something rowdy teens want, don't give it to them too soon! Make your Beloved Rascals earn the leadership reveal.

At the end of the period, say, "I'll tell you who the leaders are in a second. But let me make this clear. *You suggested leaders, but I picked them*. We had a nomination, not an election. The leaders will serve for two weeks. Every two weeks, you will give me new suggestions. If you think the leaders are doing a good job, then keep them. You will know who is doing a good job because they will occasionally earn you class game time. If they are not doing a good job of earning game time, you should suggest that I boot them out. But remember, my job, not yours, is to put together a group leaders I think will work best."

Sound the trumpets! Beat the drums! Listen to you!

You just established yourself, at least momentarily, as the Leader of Leaders!

Next step: reveal the list of leaders... encourage cheering. At the end of class, meet with your special kids, congratulate them, and set up times, as often as possible, when you can start leadership training. Very worst case scenario, meet with your leaders for a few minutes at the end of each period.

During leadership training, explain and model the behavior you want when you are lecturing: careful note talking, asking questions, eyes on the teacher, on task behavior. *Emphasize that their job is not to boss other kids around!* You want them to lead by their actions, not words.

Tell your leaders the pay-off. "When I see you exhibiting strong leadership behavior, I'll put points on the board. When we reach 10 points, we'll stop and play a game. This will take several days. Outside class, explain to the other kids what is going on and keep them cool about working a few days to earn a game."

On the next day, write the leaders' names on the board under the heading, Leaders Rule. Explain that 10 leadership points will lead to game playing. The rationale is simple, "The more work we get done in class, the more time we can have for games." When you see positive behavior from your leaders, praise it. Occasionally, put a point on the board.

What's the game? Why ask? No one can resist *Mind Soccer* (page 64).

Continue leadership training. Introduce your special kids to the essential features of Whole Brain Teaching, the Five Rules, Class-Yes, Mirror Words, Teach-Okay, etc. Frequently, ask them to model a new technique in class. Give your leaders advance info about upcoming lessons, ask advice about others in class who might be leaders, solicit their help in drawing Outsiders into classroom activities.

Leadership training will be one of the year's most rewarding experiences for you and your special kids. They will be the ones who visit the old age home and help you with your walker.

Every two weeks, take new nominees. The students will see who is earning game points and who isn't (you don't have to put points beside the leaders' names; just put them next to the heading, Leaders Rule).

The only problem we've had with leadership training and, happily, it is solvable, is the Rogue Leader. You picked Daniel; the kids adore Daniel; Daniel will be, if he wishes, at everyone's birthday party, but he has no interest in being a classroom leader. Don't scold him. Daniel is a Prince of the Realm. Cross him and you, not he, will pay the price.

But observe Daniel carefully. Every Prince has enemies; there are certainly Outsiders who have no love for Daniel. The main reason they are Outsiders is because Daniel has no use for them in his kingdom.

Before long, you realize Raul has an Outsider following and might not mind deposing Daniel. Raul is the Renegade Prince skulking around the border of Daniel's empire.

Before the two week nomination, hold a "test vote." Ask kids, in preparation for the upcoming nomination, to list the names of leaders who have done a great job of earning game points.

The kids' votes will reveal that Daniel hasn't done squat.

Take Daniel aside and say something like the following. "Daniel, look at your numbers. Not good! It may be that this leadership thing isn't for you. You can step out at the next election, or now." Let this sink in... then drop the cruncher. "I think Raul wouldn't mind *taking your place.*"

If Daniel wants out, fine. Give him a two week furlough and, if you want, allow him one more shot. Put in Raul or not... your call. You finally are the Big Honcho. Get it?

YOU'VE BECOME THE ALPHA WOLF! As you praise leaders, put up points, encourage the class to cheer for them... *you are controlling your leaders' popularity.* Everyone loves Mind Soccer. Everyone loves a leader who earns Mind Soccer points. You control the Love Machine.

There is no more valuable coin in a teenager's world, than the Golden Coin of Popularity. Your game points are a bagful of Popularity Coins. Distribute them according to your followers' merits: the kingdom has passed into your wise, gracious hands.

The key to leadership training is to be sure that there are plenty of lively lessons to learn. As the year unfolds, introduce the following to your leaders before you try each in class: the Super Improvers Team, the Scoreboard, Genius Ladder, SuperSpeed 1000, SuperSpeed Math (if you teach math), Short Talk/Long Talk/Plan Together, Please/Okay/La La, Solo Yes.

Expand the leadership group to include more students. Train them all to be outstanding Whole Brain Teachers. Have lunch together. Eating with you turns a meal into a feast. Look around the lunch room. See if you can find a Round Table, fit for the gathering of educational royalty.

CHAPTER 12

A Curriculum of Games

*Do not keep children to their studies
by compulsion, but by play.*

—PLATO

By now, you've grasped our key idea. Whole Brain Teaching is, first day to last, One Big Game. In traditional education, long work periods are broken up by short games, hours of boredom are interspersed with moments of joy. In WBT, long games are broken up by short games, quiet recreations are interspersed with hilarious contests.

Our educational philosophy can be stated in a sentence:
Kids are happiest and learn the most when they are playing.

The games in this book engage our students' whole brains, prefrontal cortex (planning), motor cortex (moving), Broca's area (speech production), Wernicke's area (understanding language), visual cortex (seeing) and the limbic system (emotions). When teachers complain that their kids don't care about a lesson, have no interest in fractions or Aborigines, what they mean, in terms of brain structure, is that their students' limbic systems, their emotions, are disengaged. Our answer? Play hard. Learn more.

Watch kids joyfully burst out of a traditional classroom at recess and you're witnessing limbic system liberation. On the playground, students' entire brains are passionately involved in seeing, speaking, hearing, moving... having as much fun as possible before the Bell of Doom. Back in the classroom, students do exactly what they don't want to do, sit still and be quiet. Traditional education is the perfect system if you like to scold kids for being kids.

Think of your classroom as an indoor playground. In WBT, students play all day without realizing how hard they're working or how much they are learning. We stitch every classroom activity together with the Golden Thread of Fun.

Your next step? Begin to create a unified teaching system with some of our largest, most powerful games.

Individual motivation: Reward and nourish individual growth with stars on the Super Improver wall.

Group motivation: Employ the multi-level Scoreboard as an endlessly engaging, classroom management game.

Critical Thinking: Use Brainies to teach a cartoon sign language that vivifies and enlivens careful thought.

Writing: Explore the wonders of the Triple Whammy, a single sentence that unfolds into an essay.

Math/Reading: Set up a weekly schedule of our SuperSpeed games in math and language arts, using personal record setting to powerfully motivate students to master basic skills.

Academic Review: Discover Mind Soccer merriment; turn weekly summaries into hilarious, race against the clock, contests.

If I had to pick a Game of Games, a yearlong, classroom unifying entertainment, it would be the Super Improvers Team (with Grit stars). In earlier chapters, I've noted how Super Improver stars can be awarded on the Scoreboard and for personal growth with Brainies, the Triple Whammy, SuperSpeed games, and Mind Soccer.

The best sign you can have in your class?

We can break any record we set.

WBT Online Resources

I f you would like a Whole Brain Teaching mentor, explore the Facebook WBT Certification pages for each grade level.

1. WholeBrainTeaching.com (our main website)
2. Youtube.com/ChrisBiffle (a collection of 90+ WBT classroom videos)
3. Facebook/Whole-Brain-Teaching
4. Facebook/wbtkindercertification
5. Facebook/wbt-1st-grade-certification
6. Facebook/wbt-2nd-grade-certification
7. Facebook/wbt-3rd-grade-certification
8. Facebook/wbt-4th-grade-certification
9. Facebook/wbt-5th-grade-certification
10. Facebook/wbtMiddleSchoolCertification
11. Facebook/wbt-High-School-Certification
12. WBTBookClub.blogspot.com (begin your quest for WBT certification here)
13. Manual: "Whole Brain Teaching for Challenging Kids" Amazon. com, http://goo.gl/NSLOQ

Webcasts

In the middle of the homepage at WholeBrainTeaching.com, each one hour webcast reviews, in detail, a key WBT strategy.

556: Overview of WBT http://goo.gl/P1GygH

557: Class-Yes and other Attention Getters http://goo.gl/oZ4Jo3
"Whole Brain Teaching for Challenging Kids," Chapter 6
Class-Yes

558: Mirror Words and other Mirrors http://goo.gl/ZkMc4T
"Whole Brain Teaching for Challenging Kids," Chapter 12
Mirror, Hands and Eyes

559: Five Rules (1), (2) http://goo.gl/xI4c9L
"Whole Brain Teaching for Challenging Kids," Chapter 7 Five,
Powerful classroom Rules

560: Implementing the Five Rules http://goo.gl/CFy4OS

561: Teach-Okay http://goo.gl/xTSVqe
"Whole Brain Teaching for Challenging Kids," Chapter 8
Teach-Okay

562: Scoreboard variations http://goo.gl/dtV84D & http://goo.gl/DG8sPK
"Whole Brain Teaching for Challenging Kids, "Chapter 11
Scoreboard & Chapter 14 Scoreboard Levels

563: Super Improver Team http://goo.gl/c1n1JO & http://goo.gl/iqCyqf
"Whole Brain Teaching for Challenging Kids," Chapter 15 The
Super Improvers Team and Chapter 16 Improving State Test
Scores with The Super Improvers Team

564: Review http://goo.gl/AmksnO

565: Practice Cards http://goo.gl/ZRTfSs
"Whole Brain Teaching for Challenging Kids," Chapter 17
Practice Cards

568: Bulls Eye Game http://goo.gl/zXdANh
"Whole Brain Teaching for Challenging Kids," Chapter 21 The
Bull's Eye Game

Pinterest

http://www.pinterest.com/wbteachers/wbt-basics/
http://www.pinterest.com/wbteachers/wbt-cool-stuff/
http://www.pinterest.com/wbteachers/wbt-levels/
http://www.pinterest.com/wbteachers/wbt-writing/
http://www.pinterest.com/wbteachers/wbt-superspeeds/
http://www.pinterest.com/wbteachers/wbt-powerpix/
http://www.pinterest.com/wbteachers/super-improvers-team/

APPENDIX B

WBT Grade Level Videos

KINDERGARTEN

WBT: Amazing Kindergarten Writing
http://goo.gl/hsEOT3

Watch in amazement as Andrea Schindler's inner city, San Bernardino, California kindergarteners demonstrate all the steps necessary for them to produce five paragraph, college style essays. You'll learn about college talk, baby talk, mirror words, air punctuation, the because clapper and the astonishing powers of the Triple Whammy sentence.

WBT: Kindergarten, "Class Rules"
http://goo.gl/mHSn4X

Watch veteran Whole Brain Teacher Andrea Schindler demonstrate a variety of lively teaching techniques while reviewing classroom rules.

WBT: Kindergarten (Expanded!)
http://goo.gl/VCq29C

Watch this substantial addition to Andrea Schindler's kindergarten video as her students demonstrate an amazing variety of Whole Brain Teaching techniques: class-yes, hands and eyes, teach-okay, switch, Mighty Oh Yeah, lines-lines-lines, seats-seats-seats, a bubble in your mouth and the wonderful crisscross applesauce!

FIRST GRADE

WBT: Starting WBT With 1st Graders
http://goo.gl/qvxTzw

Karly Macaleese, a rising WBT All Star, demonstrates how to start Whole Brain Teaching with a class of Ohio 1st graders. In only a few minutes, the kids quickly learn the Scoreboard, Mighty Groan, Mighty Oh Yeah, Class-Yes, Mirror Words and Rule 1.

WBT: 1st Grade Transitions
http://goo.gl/jb5ICR

Deb Weigel, Arizona teacher and one of Whole Brain Teaching's 2010 interns, guides her class through a masterful sequence of morning routines... five activities with smooth transitions in less than 7 minutes! Lots of WBT techniques on display, including: Five Class Rules, Class-Yes, Teach-Okay, 10 finger woo, Scoreboard, Hands and Eyes, Switch. Note the use of a student leader, the syllable chant as kids move to the back of the classroom, and the brief practice using "because," a key term in critical thinking.

WBT: 4 Minute Competition Brainy: 1st Grade
http://goo.gl/qCBnVC

Farrah Shipley's astonishing 1st graders rip through a five paragraph, oral essay on summer, inserting (non-memorized) quotations on the fly! Scoring: new paragraph (2), Triple Whammy (2), capital letter (1), because (1), and (1), period (1), capital letter proper noun (1), deep citation (15), adder (5), adder (5), compare (3), connect (5), deep citation (15), in conclusion (2). Total score = 60 points.

SECOND GRADE

WBT: Brainies in 2nd Grade
http://goo.gl/xIpfWg

Nancy Stoltenberg, Whole Brain Teaching's Director of Certification, guides her lively Palmdale, California second graders through a review of three books they have read. Note the children's delightful engagement as they use WBT's new Brainies, gestures for writing and critical thinking, to create an energetic, literary summary.

WBT: Classroom Tour 2nd Grade
http://goo.gl/n7NBMC

In one of WBT's most ambitious videos, Nancy Stoltenberg, WBT Executive Board member, presents a detailed description of first and second day activities in a Whole Brain classroom. Coverage includes: Class-Yes, Mirror Words, Switch, Rule 1, the 3-Peat, Scoreboard, Super Improvers, Power Pix, Practice Cards, the Universal Homework Model, Volume-O-Meter, seating arrangement , and wall displays. Especially useful is Nancy's step-by-step guide to implementing Teach-Okay, a core WBT strategy.

WBT 2nd Grade: 5 Step Critical Thinking Lesson with Explanatory Comments
http://goo.gl/YWaO4s

A tour de force of Whole Brain Teaching, this superb lesson by Nancy Stoltenberg, Director of WBT Certification, demonstrates an impressive array of WBT techniques. Facing a daunting instructional challenge, Nancy presents a critical thinking lesson on prediction to a group of second graders making mini-volcanoes in a sandbox! Fully annotated with explanatory comments, you'll note in this lesson; class-yes, teach-okay, mirror, mirror words, the Scoreboard, core vocabulary, memory gestures, the quick test, Triple Whammy writing, topic sentences, the because clapper, "all eyes on...", "you're still cool," air punctuation... an amazing range of tightly WBT strategies.

THIRD GRADE

Third Graders' 1st Encounter With WBT: Unedited Video!
http://goo.gl/LYuVA9

Ever wonder how to begin Whole Brain Teaching? In this remarkable video, Karly Macaleese, a rising WBT All Star, introduces a third grade class to Whole Brain Teaching. These Ohio students had brief encounters with WBT nine months earlier, but had been taught throughout the school year with traditional instructional techniques. Note the ease with which Karly introduces core WBT techniques, Class-Yes, Mirror, Mirror Words, the Scoreboard and Teach-Okay ... an engaging demo of how to start a class on a wonderful Whole Brain Teaching journey. Great teacher... amazing kids!

WBT: 3rd Grade, Math Critical Thinking

Kate Bowski

http://goo.gl/FSDK6P

Kate Bowski's energetic Delaware 3rd graders demonstrate a variety of Whole Brain Teaching skills: class-yes, teach-okay, mirrors, hands and eyes, the Scoreboard and oral writing. Especially intriguing is their use of WBT's Mind Giant cartoon characters, Biffy Bluebird who challenges them with a set of increasingly complex questions involving comparing and contrasting multiplication and addition. The video finishes with several students making remarkable mental leaps, comparing main idea and details with multiplication's factors and products.

WBT: 3-Minute Competition Brainies

Lindsey Roush 3rd Grade

http://goo.gl/yp7nTc

Watch Lindsey Roush's lively, Ohio 3rd graders create a Competition Brainy essay on geometric solids. Scoring: capital letter (1), Triple Whammy (3), contrast (3), because (1), period (1), quotation (15), quotation (15), compare (3), adder (5), adder (5), new paragraph (2), in conclusion (2), and (1) = 57 points. Two uncorrected errors, -5 each. Final score = 47 points.

WBT: 3rd Grade, Science

http://goo.gl/I7udU3

Lindsey Roush's Ohio 3rd graders demonstrate one of crucial Common Core skills, answering text based questions... while they have a blast! Whole Brain Teaching techniques demonstrated include: class-yes, teach-okay, mirror, mirror words, the Scoreboard, the Because Clapper and, a new favorite, Disguise Cream.

FOURTH GRADE

WBT: 4th Grade: The Crazy Professor Reading Game

http://goo.gl/Nvz2Fq

See Whole Brain Teaching Co-Founder, Chris Rekstad, demonstrate powerful classroom management techniques for developing reading comprehension! One of WBT's first and most popular videos.

WBT: 3 Minute Competition Brainy

Jackie Nessuno 4th grade

http://goo.gl/j2YoPX

Can your class top Jackie Nessuno's, New Jersey, 4th graders? Here's their oral essay on the Solar System for the 3 Minute Competition Brainy contest. Scoring: new paragraph (2), capital letter (1), proper noun capital (1), because (1), period (1), for example (2), but (3), simile (5), comma (1), also (2), deep citation (15), in conclusion (2). Total = 36 points.

FIFTH GRADE

WBT: 5th Grade: The Genius Ladder

http://goo.gl/q3zYLO

Watch in amazement as Jasselle Cruz's inner city, Philadelphia 5th graders use the power of the Genius Ladder to explore grammar and construct complex sentences ... a remarkable demonstration of students passionately engaged in learning... while having a blast!

WBT: 5th Graders Create 5 Paragraph ORAL Essay!

http://goo.gl/XhOfgN

Jasselle Cruz's inner city Philadelphia 5th graders attempt the impossible... spontaneously creating an oral essay on a topic they have never seen... with each student rapidly tossing in a sentence. They even create imaginary research to support each of their main points! Note not only the lively inventiveness of these great kids but also their essay's perfectly organized structure: introduction, body and conclusion.

SIXTH GRADE

WBT: 6th Grade Science

http://goo.gl/xFGj52

Sarah Meador's 6th graders give a wonderful demonstration of one of Whole Brain Teaching's most powerful potions, Disguise Cream. Her science students transform themselves into planets and stars!

WBT 6th Grade: Test Review
http://goo.gl/E5NVKP
In this award winning video, Sarah Meador's Illinois 6th graders demonstrate a lively variety of Whole Brain Teaching techniques: Class-Yes, Teach-Okay, Mirror-Words, the Scoreboard and Yes/No Way. In addition, look for some original twists on WBT standards... especially note the Winnebago Zoop!

SEVENTH GRADE

WBT: 7th Grade Science
http://goo.gl/rmi8IR
In this blockbuster, 26 minute video, Andre Deshotel's Louisiana middle schoolers demonstrate the marvels of WBT's 5 Step Lesson: Question, Answer, Exploration, Test, Critical Thinking. Also on display are a host of WBT techniques: Class-Yes, Teach-Okay, the Scoreboard, Hands and Eyes, switch, the Because Clapper, Mirror Words. Of special interest are two new, highly engaging strategies: vocab candy and disguise cream. Toward the end of the video, watch as students take over the class and teach a beat box rhythm!

WBT: 3 Minute Competition Brainy
Andre Deshotel 7th Grade
http://goo.gl/77Qmge
In one of the first Competition Brainy videos, Andre Deshotel's Louisiana 7th graders dive into an oral essay on ways in invasive species destroys an ecosystem. The score a total of 24 points. Note the following Brainies: new paragraph, capital, period, colon, Triple Whammy topic sentence, help me, for example, simile, because, detail adder, comma.

WBT 7th Graders Run Wild with Disguise Cream!
http://goo.gl/cj3i2E
In some of the most electric videos in the WBT library, Andre Deshotel's Louisiana 7th graders demonstrate Whole Brain Teaching's marvelous strategies for student engagement. In the current video, his high-

energy kids use Disguise Cream (you have to see it!) to enact varieties of symbiotic relationships. Students speak paragraphs complete with examples, air punctuation and "cool facts."

WBT: Brainies in Middle School Science
http://goo.gl/teh1Bp
Louisiana WBT All Star, Andre Deshotel, guides his energetic seventh graders through an all stops out, high-energy review of core concepts in life science! Note the use of Whole Brain Teaching's Brainies, entertaining gestures that develop students' writing and critical thinking skills.

HIGH SCHOOL

WBT: High School Math
http://goo.gl/mtTGUh
Mike Brown of Tennessee uses a masterful, low-key approach while leading his high school students through a sequence of trigonometry lessons. Note the variety of Whole Brain Teaching strategies employed: class-yes, teach-okay, mirror, memory gestures, switch, classroom rules ... even a WBT technique for rapidly passing out papers!

WBT: High School Math
http://goo.gl/KMBzJF
Watch Kristin Dewitt, veteran Whole Brain Teacher, use Class-Yes, Mirror Words, Teach Okay and a lively sense of humor as she guides her class through a lively algebra lesson.

COLLEGE

WBT: College: Classroom Management
http://goo.gl/zlOxnS
The longer we talk, the more students we lose. Chris Biffle demonstrates micro-lecturing, the crucial Whole Brain Teaching classroom management technique that not only breaks information into understandable chunks, but also has a built in check for student comprehension.

WBT: Advanced Techniques
http://goo.gl/e4zdwC

Chris Biffle, co-founder of Whole Brain Teaching (WBT), demonstrates several lively WBT techniques with his Introduction to Philosophy students.

WBT Posters

Use for Left Hand Place Value, page 114.

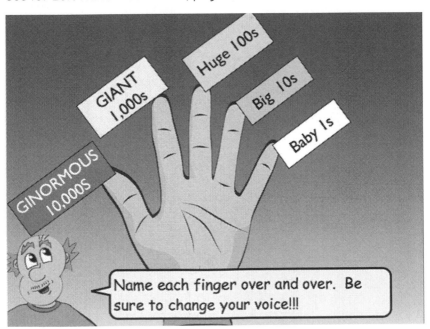

BIBLIOGRAPHY

There are a host of books on the brain, brain research and teaching. Here are nine of the best to start with.

Dweck, Carol, *Mindset,* Random House, 2006.

Freberg, Laura A., *Discovering Biological Psychology,* Wadsworth Publishing, 2009.

Greene, Ross W. *Lost at School,* Scribner, 2009.

Horstman, Judith, *The Scientific American Day in the Life of Your Brain*. Jossey-Bass, 2009.

Jones, Fred: *Tools for Teaching,* Fredric H. Jones & Associates, 2007.

Kagan, Spencer: *Collaborative Learning,* Kagan Cooperative Learning, 1994.

Kotulak, Richard, *Inside the Brain,* Andrews McMeel Publishing, 1997.

Medina, John, *Brain Rules,* Pear Press, 2008.

Restak, Richard, *The New Brain,* Rodale Books, 2003.

ABOUT THE AUTHOR

 CHRIS BIFFLE, Director of Whole Brain Teachers of America, is the author of four McGraw-Hill textbooks on critical thinking and reading. He began his teaching career in 1967 by co-founding Children's House in Watsonville, California, one of the first daycare centers in the United States for the children of migrant workers. Over the last four decades, Chris has received grants from the U.S. Department of Education, the National Endowment for the Humanities, served on the Perseus Project when it was based at Harvard, been featured on over 25 radio and television broadcasts. In 2004, Chris led the "Save Our Schools" 300 mile march on Sacramento protesting education budget cuts. He has been lead presenter at 100 Whole Brain Teaching conferences, attended by 40,000 educators. Tens of thousands of instructors across the United States and around the world base their teaching methods on his free eBooks available at WholeBrainTeaching.com.

For information about scheduling an onsite Whole Brain Teaching seminar, email ChrisBiffle@WholeBrainTeaching.com.

Notes

Made in the USA
Lexington, KY
03 July 2019